K. H. Wieser and Dr. P. V. Loiselle

# Your Garden Pond

**Practical tips on planning, design, installation and maintenance**

Acknowledgement is made to two of America's foremost aquatic nurserymen: Charles B. Thomas of Lilypons Water Gardens, Lilypons, MD 21717, and Rolf J. Nelson of Lilypons Water Gardens, Brookshire, TX 77423 for their helpful advice making this book more appropriate for American readers.
The photographs of individual ponds and water gardens used througout the book are courtesy of Stapely Water Gardens at Stapely, United Kingdom.

Library of Congress Catalog No. 85-51565
ISBN 3-923880-21-9
© 1986
**Tetra-Press**
TetraWerke Dr. rer. nat. Ulrich Baensch GmbH
P. O. Box 1580, D-4520 Melle, West Germany
All rights reserved, incl. film, broadcasting,
television as well as the reprinting

3rd edition 20.001-30.000, 1988
Printed in West Germany
Distributed in USA by
Tetra Sales (Division of Warner-Lambert)
Morris Plains, N. J. 07950
WL-Code: 16052

# Table of Contents

# Foreword to the German Edition

Many people who have a garden pond no doubt set out on the project of designing and constructing it with the best of intentions, only to find out later they have overlooked some vital point. This leads to an end result that leaves something to be desired. Needed at the onset was detailed knowledge of the necessary steps that lead to a garden pond that will eventually become a self-contained, self-regulating habitat.

Any garden pond has to be designed with proper regard to certain definitive constraints. It cannot subsequently be reduced in size, extended, or modified at whim for it is not just a transient installation to be enjoyed for a single summer. So one must be forearmed with all the necessary information before embarking on such a project. This is the only way to avoid mistakes that reduce the pleasure to be had from the pond. Nor is it simply the owner's ability as a handyman that determines success in setting up a garden pond. Equally important is an appreciation of how the water and the plants and animals in it interrelate to form a natural biotope.

In writing this book, the author aims first to set out in detail all the necessary steps involved in planning and producing a garden pond, then to give sound advice to the future owner on its subsequent maintenance. If he follows this advice, the reader will find that his garden pond will give him great pleasure in future years, will increase his intimate knowledge of the flora and fauna of such a habitat and will help provide a refuge for animals that are otherwise in a precarious state due to man's intervention.

K. H. Wieser, Melle, March 1985

# Foreword to the English Edition

When Tetra approached me with the suggestion that I edit the English translation of Dr. Wieser's excellent introduction to pond keeping, I was delighted at this opportunity to assist in making this useful work available to a broader audience. Upon initial reading, it became evident that the chapters of the original manuscript dealing with water gardening, ornamental fish and incidental inhabitants of the garden pond were of limited relevance to North American readers. Because the United States in particular spans a much greater range of climates than does Central Europe, American pond keepers enjoy many more options when planting their pools than do their German counterparts. Most European coldwater fish are unobtainable on this side of the Atlantic, while both the fishes and other aquatic animals native to North America are quite different from those found on the Eurasian land mass.

To make the English edition of *Your Garden Pond* more relevant to North American conditions, I have replaced those sections dealing with water gardening and pond residents, both permanent and incidental, with new and hopefully more apposite text and photographs. Because an introductory work such as this can only scratch the surface of such complex subjects as water lily culture or the breeding of goldfish and colored carp, I have added a brief chapter outlining means of learning more about such topics. Finally, I have appended a list of suppliers who ship water plants by mail for the benefit of readers who do not enjoy convenient access to an aquatic nursery.

Far more persons than can be recognized individually were good enough to answer questions that arose during the course of this project. However, I must acknowledge a particular debt to Patricia and Dan Fromm for information on the amphibians apt to turn up in a suburban pond, and to John Brill and Dr. David Schlesser for information on several groups of native fishes. Special thanks are in order to Rolf Nelson of Lilypons Water Garden in Brookshire, Texas, for taking time to respond to my many queries about water lily culture and bog gardening, and to his partner at Lilypons, Maryland, Charles Thomas, for allowing Tetra to use many of his lovely photographs of aquatic and bog plants as illustrations.

I can only echo Dr. Wieser's hope that this book will help prospective pond keepers to enjoy all possible success in the construction, planning and maintenance of an ecologically balanced, aesthetically satisfying garden pond.

Dr. P. V. Loiselle, Jersey City, Sept. 1986

# Introduction

This book is intended to provide the reader with all the necessary information to enable him to create his own living microcosm in a garden pond. It illustrates the wide variety of possible pond designs through the use of numerous photographs and drawings and demonstrates in detail the steps to be followed in order to set up a thriving, healthy habitat that will reward its owner with many years of pleasure.

A garden pond should constitute a genuine environment where the flora and fauna live in a mutually beneficial relationship. In order for this to happen, the pond must be designed to reflect natural conditions as closely as possible. In nature every pond or pool has marshy areas or shallow water zones, then zones of moderate depth, followed by a zone of maximum depth. A gar-

den pond should at least have, in addition to a region of deep water, a sufficiently large marshy zone to achieve this healthy, natural effect. For it is here that frogs and newts, beetles and larvae, as well as a wide range of tiny creatures and young fish, can find a refuge. It is here, too, that a number of attractive marsh plants, like iris, cattails, marsh marigolds and water arum will grow happily. The deeper waters of the pond are the home of larger fishes, water lilies and other true aquatic plants. It also serves as a retreat for the pond's inhabitants in the depths of winter when it is enclosed by a thick ice cover, as well as during the summer months when they are threatened by such predators as house cats, racoons or fish-eating birds.

# Designing and Planning the Garden Pond

### Fish Pond, Plant Pond, or a Natural Biotope

A *biotope* is a small, self-regulating area that supports its own distinctive community of plants and animals. It is quite possible for a garden pond to constitute such a community. If one offers the plants, fish, amphibians and invertebrates basic habitat conditions that suit them, then the first essential for the existence of a healthy biotope is already there. Marsh plants, beetles, dragon fly larvae and newts need a zone with a water level between 2"–8" (5–20 cm); water lilies, floating heart, lotus and the fish require a zone with a depth of at least 2 feet (60 cm). The two indeed go together to make up a whole and this in turn implies that transitional zones are possible, even desirable.

A garden pond that contains only plants could not be considered to represent a well-balanced community. Without fish to provide natural fertilizer in the form of their wastes, the aquatic plants require continuous human intervention to prosper. Furthermore, a fishless pond invites the proliferation of mosquitos, black flies and other bothersome insects, for its predator-free waters are an ideal breeding ground for these pests. A fish pond without higher aquatic plants requires continual application of algicides to maintain suitable viewing conditions. Equally important, if no hideaways are provided, the pond will hold no attraction for frogs, newts, dragon fly larvae and beetles. Neither will the fish be induced to spawn.

### Planning

The better a garden pond is planned in advance, the less work it will demand at a larger stage. The pond will become more beautiful over time and its owner will derive greater pleasure and satisfaction from it.

There are certain pre-requirements that have to be met when selecting a pond site and choosing its design:

* A garden pond that does not see the sun will never thrive. Even plants that can take partial sun require a *minimum* of 3 hours of sunlight a day, while most waterlilies will not bloom satisfactorily unless they receive at least 5 hours of sun daily.

* It must be sited as far as possible away from trees, for falling leaves and seeds collect in the water and cause pollution.

* Water has a magical attraction for small children. The areas around the edges must be designed and graduated where necessary to eliminate any danger to children.

* A garden pond ought to have a surface area of *at least* 18–25 ft$^2$ (6–8 m$^2$) if ever it is to settle down into a healthy biotope.

The following should be taken into account at the planning stage:

* The garden pond should be sited where it can be seen easily, that is, from a terrace or seats on a patio.

* The larger the pond is, the more natural it becomes. Nevertheless, it should still fit in harmoniously with the rest of the garden.

* The soil can be used to landscape the area around the pond or to construct a waterfall.

* Heavy rainfall will cause the pond to fill up to its limit. It makes sense to install a proper overflow in case water running over the edges of the pond could cause damage to the areas around it.

* A garden with a natural slope lends itself very well to the installation of a waterfall or some other running water feature.

### Basic Design Options

Essentially, there are four different options to choose from when designing a pond. Their advantages and disadvantages may be summed up as follows:

### Clay-bottomed garden ponds

This option should only be considered for sites where the depth of topsoil-preferably of a clayey nature-extends down far enough, for there is no guarantee of any kind of reliable, permanent seal on sites where the subsoil is permeable-even if one applies a sealing layer of clay up to 8"–12" (20–30 cm) thick. Nor does a clay seal afford adequate protection against the growth of underground roots or the incursions of burrowing mice and moles. Further-

more, clay-lined garden ponds must be dressed with an additional unbroken layer of sand or gravel, at least 4″ (10 cm) thick. This serves to prevent water turbidity caused by the fish digging in the bottom.

## Concrete ponds

It takes a genuine expert to construct a concrete pond that will withstand the rigors of many years of winter weather. Concrete ponds are also vulnerable to damage from even moderate seismic activity. This limits their appeal in many areas where winter weather is not a serious problem, such as California. Sealing agents need to be added to the concrete mix and structural steel reinforcements are required, whose strength must take into account the overall pool size. A framework is necessary in cases where steep banks are desired. Damage from ice can only be prevented by the incorporation of sloping walls into the design. Both financial outlay and the labor involved are substantial while the scope of possible designs is limited. Nor should one overlook one final disadvantage: concrete ponds can only be removed with pneumatic drills!

## Pre-molded plastic ponds

These ready-made ponds are constructed from heat-molded plastic. They are completely water-tight, durable enough to survive winter weather and available in all shapes, sizes and depths. However, the job of installing a pre-molded pond must be untertaken with utmost care. The liner has to fit very snugly onto a sand bed prepared in advance to provide uniform support on all sides. This is why pre-molded plastic ponds are not suitable for sloping sites. However, their main disadvantage is that their shapes do not generally lend themselves to the formation of an integrated aquatic biotope since they rule out the possibility of incorporating a marshy zone into the final layout. As noted, this significantly reduces the options available to both plants and fish.

## PVC lined ponds

From the standpoint of price, labor and most importantly, the objective of creating a natural habitat, the use of PVC liners represents the best alternative for creating a garden pond. To this end, however, one should only consider using special low emollient, ultraviolet resistant PVC sheeting *at least* 0.8 mm thick. A pond liner should be black on the side that faces the water surface and may have a granular surface texture. So-called building-grade polytheylene sheets are totally unsuitable. This material is cheap, but it ages very quickly. It then becomes brittle and tears easily. PVC liners enable construction of a pond to whatever design the builder likes. As they can be bought in a range of popular sizes, they also afford considerable flexibility in selecting the size of a garden pond. These liners have so many advantages compared to the previous construction alternatives listed that the advice given herein is based on the assumption that the reader has selected this option for constructing a pond.

*Tetra's heavy-duty, flexible PVC liner.*

# From Planning to Practice

The first pieces of equipment to procure are a pen and a quadrille ruled writing pad. Start by making a quick sketch, roughly to scale, of the overall layout of the garden: house, patio, flower beds and trees. Next, draw in a garden pond in the desired position, size and shape. Alternatively, using a range of small cut outs of ponds in various shapes (e.g., round, oval, kidney-shaped) and sizes, experiment by siting them in a variety of positions in the garden until a suitable fit is obtained. It doesn't take long to determine which best fits the existing garden layout. Having indentified the desired shape and the best possible position in the garden, mark out the future pond by staking out little wooden pegs in the ground and then joining them up to show the outline with twine The visual impression of size that the pond makes will eventually be reduced by the bank zone. However, this bank zone is not only desirable in the sense that it gives a natural look to the edge of the pond but, being a marsh, it provides a home for many particularly attractive plants and it interesting animals.

It was stated at the outset that a garden pond should not be less than 18 ft$^2$ (6 m$^2$) in size and if at all possible, larger. Using this minimum figure as a starting point in the case of an oval pond, the following dimensions result:
Length: approx. 9 ft (3.0 m)
Width: approx. 7$^3$/$_4$ ft (2.50 m)
Depth to be excavated for the water zone: at least 30" (c. 80 cm)
Depth to be excavated in the marshy zone 2" (c. 30 cm)
Ratio of water to marshy zone 2 : 1
Pond edge: 8"–12" (c. 20–30 cm)
Given these conditions, the side walls fall away at an angle of 55°–60°. But if the pond is made just one metre longer and broader, the angle of inclination (gradient) of the side walls is only 45°.
A round pond with a diameter of 9 ft (c. 3 m) has a surface area of about 2 ft$^2$ (c. 7 m$^2$), whereas one with a diameter of 12 ft (c. 4 m) comes to 39 ft$^2$ (c. 12.5 m$^2$) and a 15 ft (c. 5 m) diameter pond amounts to 60 ft$^2$ (c. 20 m$^2$). The figures illustrate clearly that it pays to plan for a pond of generous proportions.

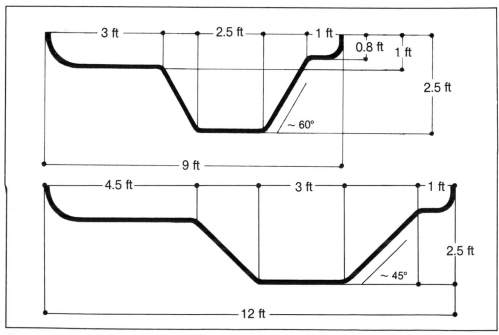

*Properly laid out, even a simply designed oval pond such as this can accomodate a marsh zone along its margins.*

## What is the Best Time to Build a Pond?

The answer depends upon both the timing of the spring thaw in a given area and the availability of the plants to be cultivated. Before May and after September the selection of aquatic plants on sale at nurseries, garden centers and aquarium shops is limited. After October the growing season is too brief to allow the plants to become sufficiently well established before the onset of winter north of Zone 10. The earthmoving work should thus be started as soon as the ground can be worked. However, final planting and subsequent filling of the pool with water should not take place before late spring and must at all events be completed by early autumn.

## Should a Power Cable Be Laid?

Basically, the answer is always yes. Whether the eventual intent is to illuminate the adjacent terrace, install a fountain, build a waterfall or put in a filter, power is essential. An electrical cable and associated connections should always be fitted by a licensed electrician to necessary safety standards. Useful tip: a photograph or a sketch of the cable track will greatly facilitate locating its precise position even a number of years later. Such information will prove useful if further landscaping or construction work is ever undertaken in that part of the yard.

## How to Make the Garden Pond Safe For Children

Water attracts children like a magnet. For this reason it is essential to take all necessary precautions to avoid accidents. In the extreme case, this would entail suspending a net over the pond's surface or erecting a fence around it! However, if the area around the pond is designed with care, it will not only look better but also reflect accurately the conditions encountered in such a biotope while satisfying the requirements of child safety.

The area enclosing the deep water zone of the pond should be laid out as a shallow bank zone about 1½ ft (c. 50 cm) wide. Then excavate this zone to a depth of about 8"–12" (c. 20–30 cm) and landscape it with boulders, rocks and bogwood right up to the edge of the deep water zone. The intervening spaces can be filled with coarse gravel in some spots, fine gravel in others. Low growing plants can now be set out in the foreground, with medium-high to tall plants at the rear. This landscaped buffer zone serves to keep small children well away from the potentially dangerous deep end of the pond.

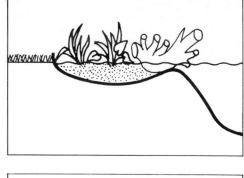

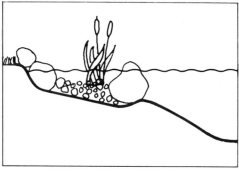

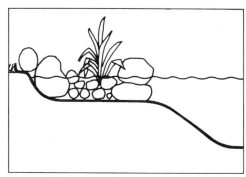

## Summary

A garden pond needs 4–6 hours of sunshine a day.

Do not site it close to trees.

Aim to construct the largest possible size pond that will suit the garden.

The marshy zone should take up about one-third of the total area.

Always take precautions to ensure that children cannot fall in.

Excavation depths:

Marshy zone: to approximately 1 ft (c. 30 cm)

Medium water zone: 1¾–2 ft (c. 50–60 cm)

Deep water zone: 2–3 ft (c. 80–90 cm)

Area around the edge: Width: 8"–20" (20–50 cm)

Depth: 8"–12" (c. 20–30 cm)

Consider all these points carefully before excavating the first spadeful of soil.

*Above: Obstacles like boulders, rocks and bogwood can prevent children from coming close to the deep water zone.*

*Opposite and following pages: These sketches suggest several possibilities for situating a pond in a back yard garden.*

# Constructing a Garden Pond

## Excavating the Basin

The following tools are necessary to build a garden pond: spade, shovel, rake, wheelbarrow, a long batten, spirit level or hose leveling instrument and a tape measure. Start by marking the outline of the deep water zone of the future pond with small pegs driven into the ground. Then stake out the shape of the transitional or marginal and the marshy zones in the same way. These marker pegs should convey an exact idea of the size of each zone. They also make it easier to keep to the depths originally envisaged once digging begins. Start digging at the pond's projected deepest point and work methodically outwards towards the outlined margins. First remove the turf if the site is on a lawn. Otherwise remove the top layer of soil to a depth of 6" (c. 15 cm). For the moment, leave the marginal zone and the marsh area undisturbed. At the center of the deep water zone, excavate relatively sharply sloping sides until the desired depth of at least 30" (c. 80 cm) has been reached. Then extend the pit for the pond proper gradually outwards towards the sides. Remember, the angle of repose for the walls of this deep water zone should not exceed 60°. At this point, refrain from any attempt to shape the final contours of the side walls. First excavate the marshy zone to a depth of 12" (c. 30 cm). This can then be sloped gradually to a depth of 18"– 24" (c. 50–60 cm) in the

*Ponds are not only attractive in large gardens. These three examples show that ponds fit very well into small, narrow yards. Close to a terrace or an additional bench these ponds will give joy and satisfaction to their owners. Do not believe ponds have no place in a small garden. These drawings prove the opposite.*

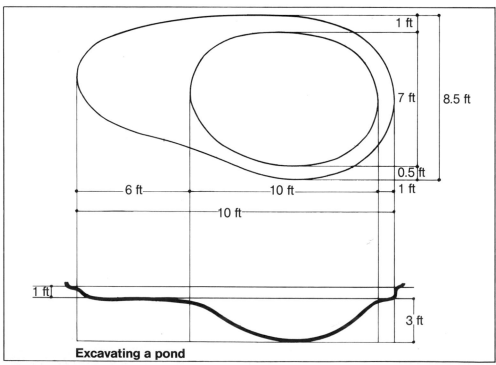

**Excavating a pond**

*Above: Zones of the pond: top view and cross section.*
*Opposite: Seven sketches how to excavate a pond and to locate the different zones. Make your own sketch before excavation!*

**Excavation depths**

M    = Marsh  zone         (to app. 1 ft.)
E    = Edge zone           (to app. 1 ft.)
Me  = Medium water zone (1¾–2 ft.)
D    = Deep water zone    (2–3 ft.)

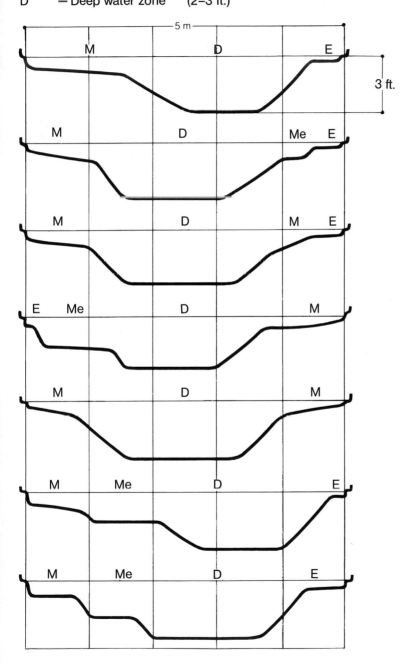

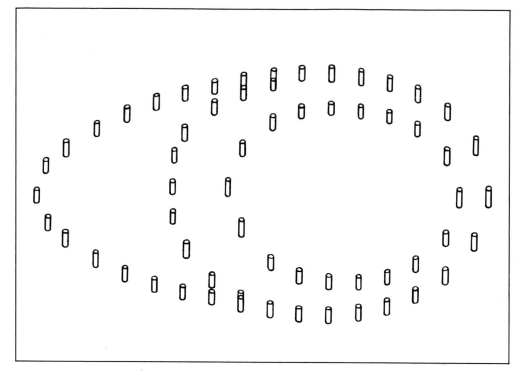

*Mark the zones of your planned pond. A precise layout prevents mistakes by showing the eventual shape of your garden pond.*

intended transitional zone. During the course of all these operations it is absolutely essential to check continually on the depths attained. This is particularly important in the marshy and transitional zones, where the soil must ultimately bear considerable localized weight. Undisturbed soil makes a much better foundation for heavy objects such as rocks than an area that has been backfilled and tamped down.

After the transitional zone has been excavated to its final depth, the sides of the deep water zone can then be finished off to slope evenly and gradually from its edges. Once all the rough excavation has been completed, the marshy zone can be laid out. Remember to ensure that it has a constant depth and width and, above all, a level base.

This is essential to the success of eventual efforts to landscape it with rocks, wood, plants and gravel. Now level the pond bottom with the rake. Aim for an even, smooth surface. Backfill any depressions with well-tamped loam, clay or sand.

Now check the whole surface **by hand** for any protruding sharp objects. Good pond liners are very elastic and tear-resistant. However, they can be damaged by root ends and other sharp-edged objects. Hence it is necessary to conduct a thorough inspection of the pit before emplacing the liner. If the floor of the pit is indeed smooth, the pond liner can then be laid directly upon it. Otherwise, a bed of sand about .75"–1.5" (2–3 cm) thick affords good protection against damage to the liner.

*Above: Possible location of a pond in the back yard.*
*Below: Beginning the actual excavation.*

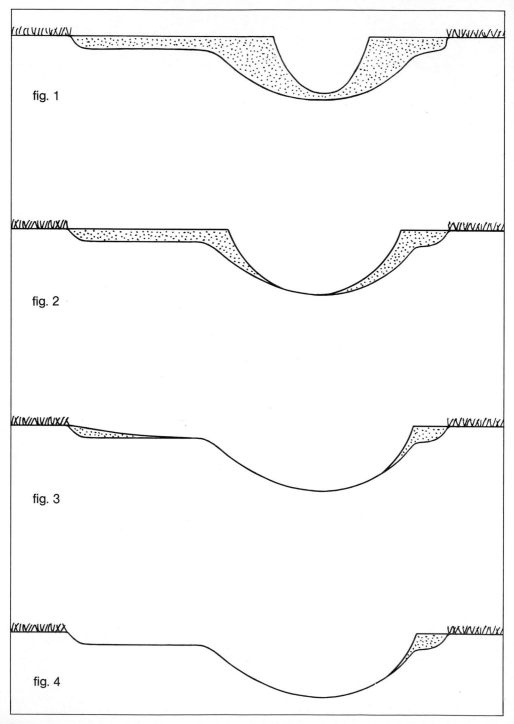

fig. 1

fig. 2

fig. 3

fig. 4

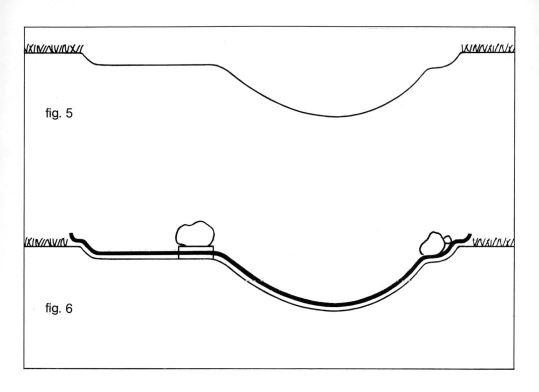

fig. 5

fig. 6

*Cross-sectional diagram showing the progressive excavation of a garden pond. Always begin by excavating the deepest portion of the pond first. It is much easier to shape and excavate the transitional and marginal zones to their proper depth if one works in this fashion.*

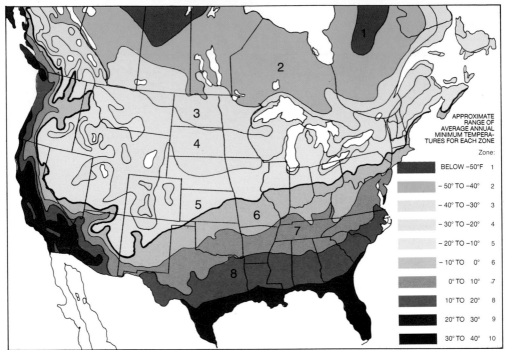

APPROXIMATE
RANGE OF
AVERAGE ANNUAL
MINIMUM TEMPERA-
TURES FOR EACH ZONE

Zone:

| | | |
|---|---|---|
| | BELOW −50°F | 1 |
| | − 50° TO −40° | 2 |
| | − 40° TO −30° | 3 |
| | − 30° TO −20° | 4 |
| | − 20° TO −10° | 5 |
| | − 10° TO 0° | 6 |
| | 0° TO 10° | 7 |
| | 10° TO 20° | 8 |
| | 20° TO 30° | 9 |
| | 30° TO 40° | 10 |

*Pondkeepers living south of the bold line will have no problem overwintering fish, if their pond is at least 30″ (80 cm) deep.*

## Some Important Design Guidelines

The marshy zone should amount to a quarter or, better still, a third of the total surface area and the transition zone should be between 8″–18″ (c. 20–50 cm) wide.

It makes sense to design a wider transition zone on the far side of the pond, for otherwise the plants and decoration would impede the view of the water. Excavate the marsh and edge zones to between 8″ and 12″ (c. 20 and 30 cm) deep and the deep water zone to at least 30″ (c. 80 cm). A water depth of 80 cm will afford protection against the pond freezing solid in those regions of North America south of the dividing line on the accompanying map. Strict adherence to this figure will ensure that fish left to overwinter in the pond will survive. The more rigorous winter climate to the north of this dividing line confronts the pond keeper with

two options. The first is to overwinter his fish inside in unheated tanks. This may be the easiest answer to severe winter weather if his fish are few in number and relatively small in size. Alternatively, the maximum depth of the pond can be increased to assure an ice-free zone. As local climatic conditions vary considerably, it is inappropriate to suggest such maximum depths herein. Contact the local office of the state or provincial Fish and Wildlife Agency and request information on the maximum thickness of lake ice in the area recorded over a ten year period. These agencies keep such records as part of their ongoing fisheries management programs and will gladly provide it on request. Addition of c. 8″ (20 cm) to the maximum figure will guarantee the fish an ice-free zone during the coldest winter.

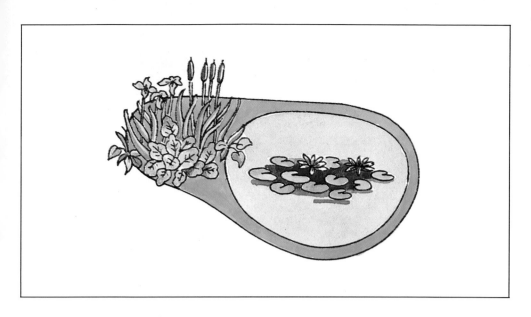

*Two different forms of ponds: a naturally shaped pond with a large marsh zone (above) and a pond bordered by the flag stones of a terrace (below).*

*A round pond (left) is suitable for any kind of garden. An oval pond (right) allows the inclusion of extensive transitional and marsh zones.*

*The design is very attractive and allows to emphasize the transitional zone. Such a pond closely approaches truly natural conditions.*

*Schematic drawing of a "child-proof" pond. Its extensive transitional zone, liberally decorated with large rocks and pieces of driftwood, effectively keeps children away from the central deep water zone.*

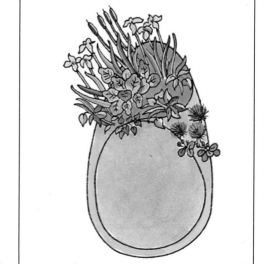

*A simply classical design for a garden pond.*

## If the Site is On a Slope

There are two possible ways of adapting a pond to suit a sloping site:

1. Install the pond in such a manner that the water level corresponds to the height of the terrain at the **lowest** point of the planned pond (Figure below). In this case the liner rests on undisturbed soil and no shifting of the subsoil is involved. This is a safe, lasting solution. The disadvantage is that the resultant water surface is somewhat smaller than might be expected, given the amount of excavation involved.

2. The water level corresponds to the highest point of the terrain. Obviously, the drop-off due to the slope must be compensated for by shifting excavated soil to the appropriate place. (Figure below). This dike of soil can eventually give way due to the action of rain and frost, combined with the pressure of the pond water. Hence such efforts to raise the ground level must be done with the utmost care. Such dikes must be carefully compacted to provide a secure base. It is advantageous if after such restructuring the land can be left to settle over the winter. This gives the new structure time to stabilize. The advantage of this method is a larger water surface for the effort expended, while part of the excavated soil can be used to construct the retaining dike. Furthermore, the view of the water from the higher side of the pond is better.

Despite these advantages, the suitability of this approach largely depends upon the nature of the soil on site. Not every soil type can be banked up with sufficient firmness. Light loams and sandy soils are not suited to such designs.

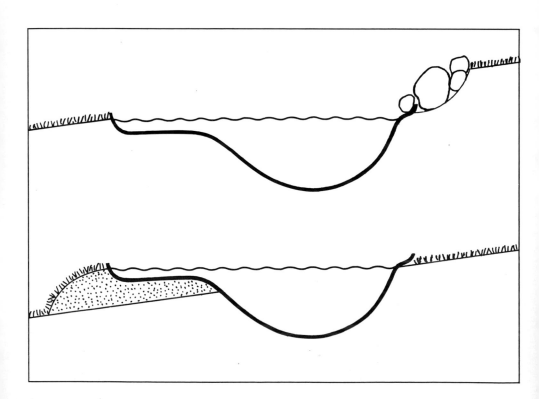

fig. 1

## How to Construct a Rectangular Pond

Idiosyncratic features of the garden layout, the location of existing seating areas or the desire to install a garden pond immediately adjacent to a terrace or patio, may necessitate the design of a rectangular pond. Garden ponds with one or more straight sides are highly susceptible to shifting of the ground in their immediate vicinity if their sides fall away steeply. A well compacted base without any heaped up soil, such as is often found close to patios is essential if the pond is to prove durable. The angle of repose of the pond walls should never exceed 60° and preferably should be as far

*The figures 1–4 show examples of rectangular ponds. It might be necessary to have one or two or three straight sides adjacent to a terrace or path. It is essential to retain a marsh zone when planning such ponds in order to retain a natural appearance.*

fig. 2

fig. 3

below this figure as practical. Remember, a marsh zone should also be incorporated into such a pond and design its layout accordingly.

If the edges are to be finished in natural stone or flagstones, the following construction technique is recommended. After lifting the last row of flagstones on the patio, lay down a concrete foundation on the exposed area. Rest the pond liner on the level surface thus provided and pull it up firmly against the second row of flagstones. Reset the row of previously lifted flagstones on the liner, either in sand or mortar. Alternatively, fix the flagstones directly onto the liner with a silicone adhesive. This will also guarantee an adequate hold. A very natural-looking effect can be achieved by holding the liner in place with a wooden beam, such as a railway tie. Bear in mind, however, that it is not possible to apply any preservatives to this beam, because such agents attack the liner. Hence only use wood that has been vacuum impregnated or beams, such as oak railway ties, that have not been freshly treated with preservative. As with flagstones, these beams serve to give the pond a straight margin. They may be used lengthways to make up a whole side or placed end on end as cut-offs on a concrete or stone foundation, with the liner under the beams turned upwards. (Figure 2). If two beams are placed parallel to one another, the liner should be pulled between the beams. (Figure 3).

fig. 4

*Opposite: Note how a railroad tie has been used to create a straight margin in this attractive pond.*

## How to Make an Overflow

Sun and wind cause the water to evaporate. On a hot day, the pond depth may drop as much as 1″ (c. 2.5 cm), whereas rain fills the pond up once more. However, heavy rainstorms can deposit so much rain so quickly the pond will overflow. If it has been properly designed, this excess water will escape from the pond at the lowest point on its rim and simply run off onto lawns, flower beds and paths. This rarely causes problems. However, there is a simple way to ensure that any surplus water will be led off to a point where it can do no harm.

All that needs to be done is to dig out a soakaway or sump close to the lowest point along the pond's rim. This is then filled with rocks, followed by stones, then pebbles and finally topped with soil or turf. The size of the soakaway will vary, depending upon the volume of the pond and on the nature of the soil. If the deeper soil strata allow water to drain away readily, then for a garden pond with a surface area of 60 ft² (c. 20 m²) a pit c. 3′ (1 metre) across and c. 3′ (1 metre) deep will suffice. To connect pond and sump, cut a round opening into the liner with a razor blade and seal the pipe connection ends on either side with an O-ring.

From this connection either a plastic pipe or a hose can be used to carry the overflow water off.

Another possibility is to build in a conduit in the form of a small ditch lined with plastic, or simply dug out, without any lining, but decorated with the occasional boulder, pieces of bogwood and the odd bog plant. The overflowing water then collects in the channel from where it will gradually drain away into the subsoil. These ditches can be made to look attractive by planting their sides with ornamental grasses or ground cover plants to make them reflect conditions along a stream bank.

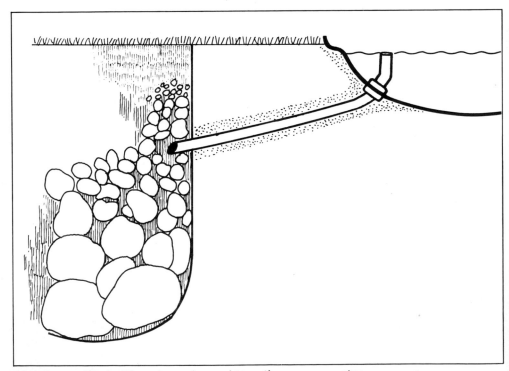

*A soakaway filled with rocks and gravel to gather excess water. Topped with soil and turf, it is effectively invisible.*

## How to Join PVC Liners

If one wishes to lay out a very large pond or else link two smaller ponds with a connecting channel, it will be necessary to join two or more PVC liners together. Builders' supply houses carry welding solutions which provide a safe and sure means of joining PVC liners without the use of heat. The only materials required for such a project are: a level, firm base; a flat paint brush about 2" (5 cm) wide; a pressure roller; 2–3 plastic bags, each filled with roughly 10 lbs (4–5 kg) of sand and sealed; and the welding solution. Spread the liners to be joined on the firm base (e.g. planking) so that they overlap by 2"–2¾" (c. 5–7 cm). Both surfaces must be thoroughly cleaned beforehand as well as **absolutely dry.** Take care during the process of arranging the weld to ensure that the liners do not slide up against one another, otherwise kinks or folds may form. Give the overlapping liner edges a good coating of the adhesive with the brush, *press* down with the roller and then hold them in position using the sandbags. Curing time depends upon air temperature. The warmer it is, the faster the cold weld becomes effective; below 65°F (18°C) it is difficult to obtain an effective seal. Move the sandbags along the seal as it is extended. It is a good idea to leave each one in place on the join for about 5–10 minutes. If only small segments of liner (up to 12" (c. 30 cm) along the margin) are to be joined under circumstances where they are not going to be subjected to any great stress, e.g. where they form the transition from the pond into a small watercourse, one can also use a special adhesive for PVC liners usually available at retail pet shops. It is also possible to join them with silicone rubber. However, the durability or robustness of the joint following use of either of these alternive methods is somewhat limited.

## Installing the Pond Liner

Once the actual pit for the pond has been dug, the real hard work is over. If the pond liner has not yet been purchased, it is now possible to work out precisely what size will be needed. Lay a line to follow the depth contours of the pond across both length and width, record its length, then add 1 ft. (c. 30 cm) onto each side. That is to say, the liner must be 2 ft (c. 60 cm) longer than the actual measurements taken for both the length and the width.

Prior to its actual emplacement in the excavation, lay the pond liner out, black side up, and let it warm in the sun. If the elements are kind, it will take no more than 30 minutes to make the liner soft and supple. But do be careful, because if the sun's rays are too intense, the liner can heat up so rapidly and to such an extent that any lawn under it will be burned. Where a fountain is planned or where placement of heavy stones is contemplated to demarcate the marshy zone from the deeper water, lay styrofoam plates 0.5"–1" (1–2 cm) thick on the floor of the excavation. Now position the pond liner over the hole so that it overlaps its edges by at least 1 ft. (c. 30 cm) all round. Weigh the center down with a couple of stones and lower the liner into the pit.

Regardless of the shape of pond chosen, folds in the liner are unavoidable. However, given a little forethought and some care during installation, these can be reduced to a minimum. Those creases that do inevitably arise should all run in the same direction if possible and preferably away from the point at which an observer will be looking at the pool. Smoothing out the creases may prove difficult in cold weather. In this case, the creased parts can be rendered more pliant by simply warming them with a hair drier. Hold the creases down with stones. **Take care to ensure that wherever a fountain is to be installed or heavy stones are to be placed subsequently, the liner lies totally flat and crease-free!** If the intent is to place a layer of planting medium in the marshy zone, rather than restrict plantings to trays or tubs, any folds must be pressed flat with stones before the medium is added. Otherwise soil or gravel particles may get between them and prevent them from ever lying down flat once the pond is filled with water. Once these operations have been completed, place additional styrofoam plates on the liner wherever the plastic will be subjected to extra heavy loading. Once this is done,

Lay a rope or hose to the required shape and size of the pool, adjusting until all aspects are satisfactory. Commence digging, but always cut inside the finished outline to allow for final trimming and shaping.

The excavating is started leaving marginal shelves where required 9" wide and 9" below water level. The pool edge should be cut back sufficiently to accommodate the edging.

Short wooden pegs are inserted 3 ft–4 ft apart around the pool and the tops levelled using a spirit level. The top edge of the pool must be levelled which is important as the water will immediately show any faults.

After final trimming and shaping has been completed, the depth and width of marginal shelves should be checked. The side and base of the excavation must be closely inspected for any sharp stones or roots.

A cushion of sand 1/2" deep should be placed on the bottom of the excavation. Sand should then be worked into the sides of the excavation to fill any holes and crevices which may have been made by digging out stones.

The finished excavation should be neat and trim as irregularities will show after the liner is fitted. On stony ground infested with weeds or roots, building grade polyethylene should be underlaid as an added precaution.

The pool liner should be draped loosely into the excavation with an even overlap all around. Stones or blocks should be placed on the corners and as required on the sides. Commence filling with water from the tap.

As the pool fills, the stones should be eased off at intervals to allow the liner to fit snugly into the excavation. Some creasing is inevitable, but some creases can be removed by stretching and fitting as the pool fills.

When the pool is full the surplus lining can be cut off leaving a 4"–5" flap. This can be temporarily secured by simply pushing 4" nails through the lining and into the ground to ensure the liner does not slip.

Rectangular pools can be edged with pre-cast paving. Informal pools can be edged with broken slabs, but natural stone paving is better. This should be laid on a bed of mortar 3 parts sand to 1 part cement.

The finished pool. Ideally pools should be emptied before planting and stocking with fish, and this is imperative if cement has been dropped into the water during the construction work.

The pool is planted and established. Fountains, lighting and other adornments can be added. In this pool a small fountain is added which will not disturb the water lilies and deep marginal plants.

decorative boulders and rocks or the support for a fountain can be placed on these reinforced spots. The edge of the liner can now be cut off around the edges to leave a "skirt" about 1 ft. (c. 30 cm) wide.

## What to Do With the Spoil

If the garden pond is sited on a lawn, the thinly cut turves can be composted. A garden pond covering an area of 30 ft$^2$ (c. 10 m$^2$), of which about one-third will be a marshy zone, results in about 15 ft$^3$ (c. 5 m$^3$) of spoil. If the subsoil is genuinely poor, a maximum of about 3–5 ft$^3$ (c. 1.0–1.5 m$^3$) of this can be used for planting medium. The remainder must either be hauled away, or alternatively used for landscaping the vicinity of the pond. If the spoil is used for landscaping, bear in mind that *raising* the levels slightly around the edges of the garden will have the effect of *visually narrowing* it. On the other hand, any mounds in the middle *tend to foreshorten* the garden. A series of low mounds behind or at the side of a pond can look very decorative if planted with the right subjects. An erratic pattern of boulders set among the plants helps to break up the design.

Grasses such as pampas grass or purple moor grass are suited to sites in full sun or semi-shade and fit in well in the vicinity of a garden pond. A word of warning: these grasses have a tendency to grow rampant and spread invasively outward from their original location. This can be avoided by planting them within a circular "collar" of aluminium or fiberglass sheet emplaced to a depth of 8″ (c. 20 cm). The upper edge of such a barrier should just protrude from the soil surface. If it proves too conspicuous, it can always be camouflaged with gravel or pebbles, but as a rule the overhanging grass leaves quickly conceal its presence. The material for such "collars" is readily available at nurseries or home and garden centers.

Do not build up any mounds of earth in the immediate vicinity of the pond's edge. Heavy rainfall can wash significant amounts of topsoil into the water creating significant turbidity. By the same token the pond should be accessible from all sides so dead and decaying plant material can be removed and any other necessary maintenance work easily carried out.

## How to Make a Waterfall

The spoil can also serve as the foundation for a waterfall. A waterfall is not merely a decorative feature. It also enriches the water with oxygen, to the benefit of both plants and fishes. The following material are needed to build a waterfall:

A pump of the appropriate capacity
An electrical outlet
A ½ to ¾ inch diameter hose
Plastic sheeting
Decorative rocks
Sheet styrofoam

There are two alternative approaches to driving a waterfall. Both entail using a centrifugal pump to raise the pond water under pressure to the highest point of the waterfall, whence it falls back into the pond basin. The first is based on the use of a submersible pump placed directly into the pond. The second depends upon a non-submersible unit mounted outside of the pond and drawing water up through an intake pipe laid on the bottom. There is little to choose between submersible and non-submersible pumps from the standpoint of throughput and pumping height. Submersible pumps are somewhat more versatile, for they can be employed without modification both to run a fountain or drain the pond. Externally mounted pumps, on the other hand, are more easily maintained.

Perhaps the most important consideration in the choice of a pump for the garden pond is its bulk. Water pumps must be fitted with a reliable, effective and easily cleaned prefilter. Algae, leaf litter and other debris must be removed from the water before it passes through the pump lest its function be seriously compromised. In a large pond, a submersible pump poses no problems, for there is more than enough room to house both pump and filter together. In a smaller pond, spatially separating filter and pump leaves more growing room for plants and swimming room for fish. Hence the advan-

*A lovely example of how much a waterfall can add to the visual impact of a garden pond.*

tage of using an externally mounted unit to power the waterfall.

The design of the waterfall determines the pump capacity required to run it. The higher the waterfall, the more effort required to lift a given volume of water to its summit. This means that the volume of water per minute pumped by a given unit depends largely upon the height to which it must be raised. The higher the waterfall, the more powerful the pump required to run it. Reliable pump manufacturers list clearly the relationship between throughput and pumping height. This information should be carefully consi-

dered both when designing a waterfall and before purchasing a pump.

A waterfall should be designed so that the water descends into the pond via a number of different steps. To create this feature, use the spoil, built up to form a small hillock and compacted as much as possible to give a really firm base. Cut the individual steps as smoothly as possible so that the liner can be laid flat on them. The water channel should be hollowed out towards the center to prevent the water from spilling over the sides. A suitable liner is then laid to fit this form as closely as possible and without any

*Use the spoil to build a small hillock for a waterfall. The steps should be shaped smoothly to accomodate the liner that will be placed on them.*

folds. In those parts where flagstones form the terracing, place a $\frac{1}{4}''-\frac{1}{2}''$ (c. 0.5–1 cm) thick styrofoam block under them. The weight of the stone compresses this block against the liner in such a way that the water does not flow under the liner but over the flagstone. Work from the bottom to the top. The bowl at the top can consist of a bed made up of pebbles or large gravel, or the hose can be led through an appropriately sized hole in a slightly inclined flagstone. The liner can then be concealed with a covering of gravel, pebbles and ornamental stones. The last step of the waterfall, where the water enters the pond, should be a large flat natural stone that juts out over the pond surface. This serves to maximize the aerating effect of the waterfall while preventing bottom scouring and stirring up of sediments.

Finally, run a heavy duty plastic hose from the pump to the top of the waterfall. Do not use lightweight flexible plastic tubing. This is made brittle by action of frost and thus tends to break easily. This quickly becomes a problem because it is necessary to clean the inside of the hose regularly with a pipe brush. It only takes a few months for a deposit of algae and other matter to form there which can drastically reduce the hose diameter. This in turn causes the throughput to fall markedly.

## How to Install a Fountain

It is often impossible to emplace a sprinkler or a fountain as an afterthought. Hence it is advisable to take the installation of such an accessory into account in the pond's planning stage. Before deciding on a fountain, bear in mind that water lilies do not appreciate being sprinkled with water all the time. Whether one includes frogs, ducks or other figures to spew out the water is strictly a matter of taste. These figures weigh very little. Hence whether they are put at the edge of the pond or in the centre, no special precautions are called for. Millstones or other drilled boulders, however, are of such great weight that they can easily damage a liner. A great deal of care is required if these are to be installed.

The site of the fountain should be determined before the pond is excavated. Excavate its bed to a depth of only c. 4″ (10 cm) below the level of the future water surface and level it carefully. This operation is obviously much simpler if the fountain is to rest in the marshy or transitional zone of the pond. Before installing the liner lay a c. $\frac{3}{4}''$ (2 cm) thick styrofoam plate on the bed. Next, place the liners in position in the hole and pull it tight over the area that will bear the fountain's weight. *Take care to eliminate any creases.* Then, on top of the liner, place another styrofoam

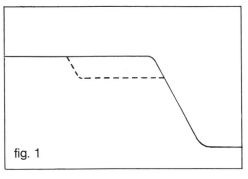

fig. 1

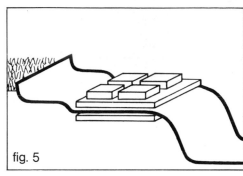

fig. 5

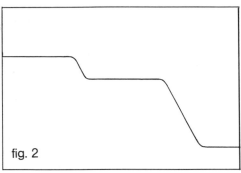

fig. 2

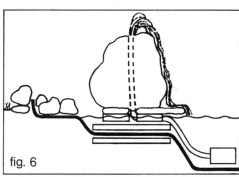

fig. 6

*Fig. 1–6: These figures show how to install a fountain. It should be installed at the very beginning because it is almost impossible to add a fountain to a pond once it has been filled.*

*The styrofoam plates protect the liner. The rocks on top are necessary as a solid base for a millstone or similarly massive source for the water's outlets.*

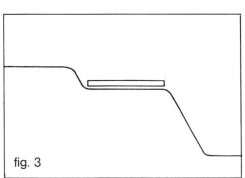

fig. 3

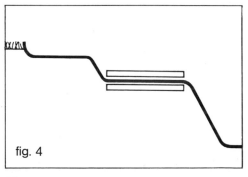

fig. 4

plate to cover the first. The bed is now ready to receive the foundation of brick or natural rock upon which the millstone or other outlet will rest. This will place the fountain's source well above the water level. Now pass the hose leading from the pump to the hole in the rock through the substructure. Since this hole does not necessarily have to correspond with the hose diameter, rubber O-rings pulled over the hose and pressed into the hole through the stone will prevent water from running back out.

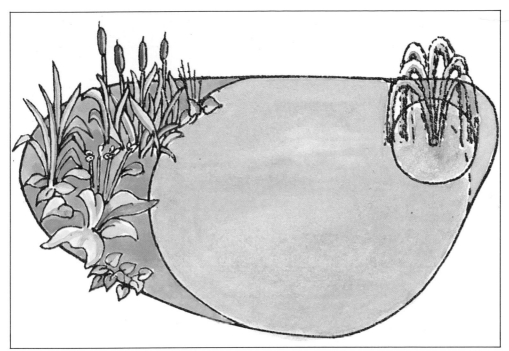

*Always place a fountain on the edge of a pond. Thus the natural growth of plants will not be disturbed.*

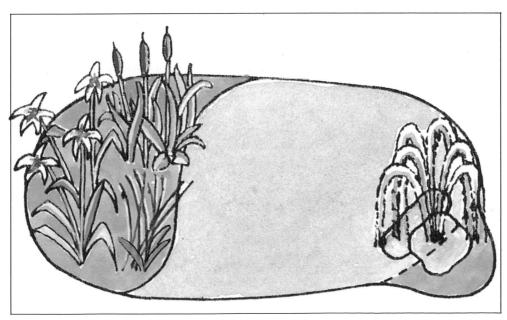

*A fountain does not need to be obstrusive to be both aesthetically and functionally affective.*

## How to Lay Out the Pond Margin

A garden pond will only appear natural if its banks and edges reflect the conditions found in the wild. A common mistake is the failure to include the pond margins — and what is to be done with them — in the overall plan. It simply detracts from the beauty of a pond if the liner is still visible around the edges. Proper layout of the margins calls for a good deal of work. It needs to be not only well thought out but also carefully put into practice. ***Once the liner has been cut off, then any amount of subsequent striving to create a natural looking marginal zone will be in vain.*** In essence there are two possible approaches to the creation of a natural pond margin:

1. The gradient of the hole dug out for the marsh and transitional zones of the pond can be made so shallow over a width of at least 2 ft (c. 60 cm) that any gravel, rocks or wood used will remain in place without any other anchorage. From this peripheral zone, whose gradient should not exceed 15°, the angle of repose of the pond walls can increase sharply to the maximum value of 60°. This method of construction without doubt most truly reflects natural conditions, but it represents a feasible and satisfactory solution only for ponds whose length and breadth exceed 15 ft (c. 5 m).

2. The bank zone is created using boulders, bogwood, pebbles, plants and gravel. Depending upon the size and shape of the pond, this edge zone can be between 8"–12" (c. 20–50 cm) wide. The really important thing is that decorative materials be solidly implanted, sufficient to ensure that they will remain in place. This means a narrow hori-

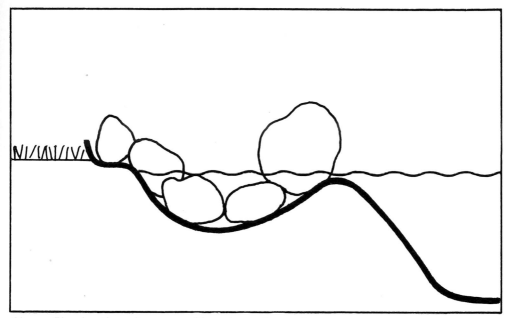

*Above: Shaping the edge zone with rocks and gravels.*

*Below: Planting low growing plants along the margin integrates the pond into its natural surrounding.*

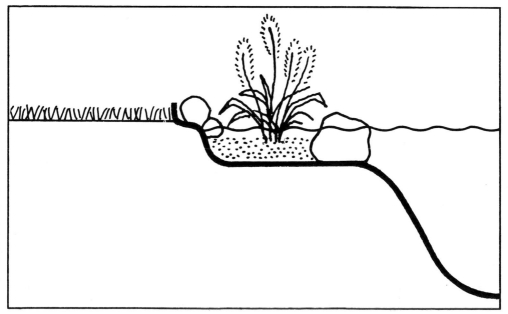

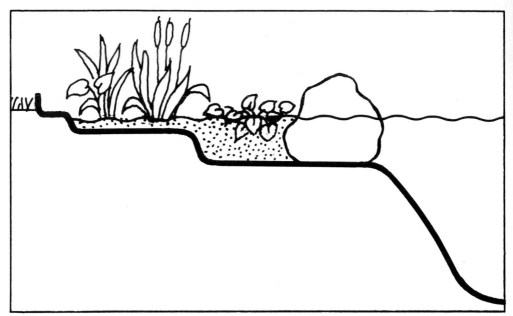

*Above: A large rock placed at the edge of the deep water zone affords a pond with a wide marsh zone capable of supporting a variety of plants.*

*Below: A flat marginal zone can be made to look more natural through the use of gravel bottom.*

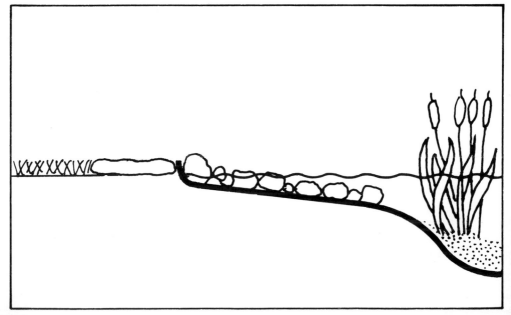

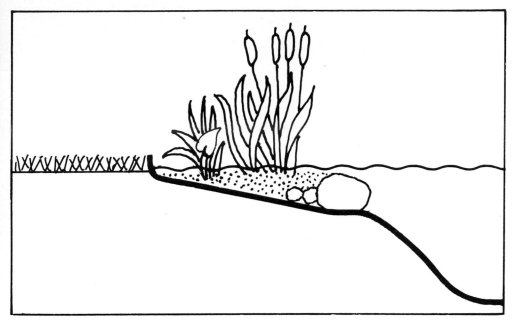

*Above: Tall plants should only be used as a background for the pond.*

*Below: Setting a plate onto the liner will prevent it from sipping after the pond is filled with water.*

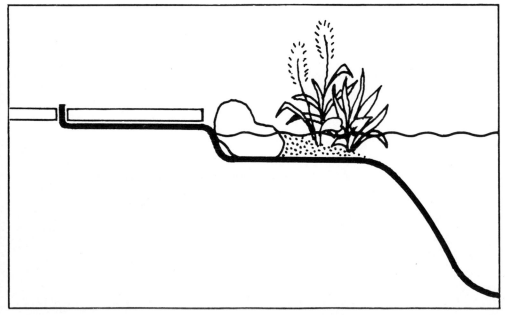

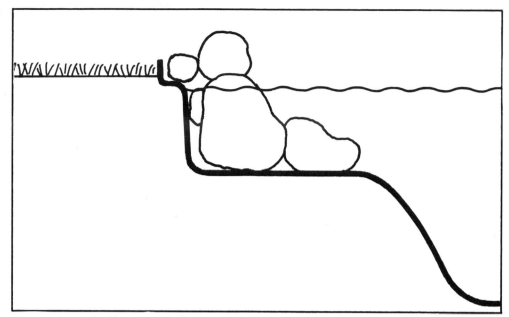

*Above: A pond without a marsh zone, possibility for large garden ponds.*

*Below: Using pieces of wood to decorate the marsh zone makes the pond look natural because moss will grow on the wet wood.*

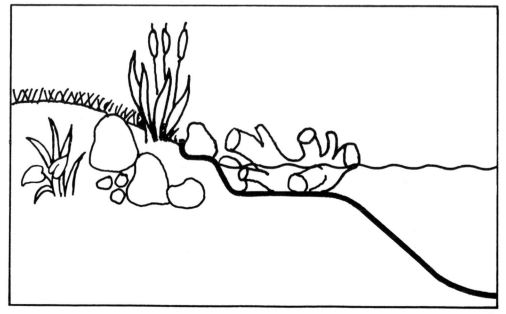

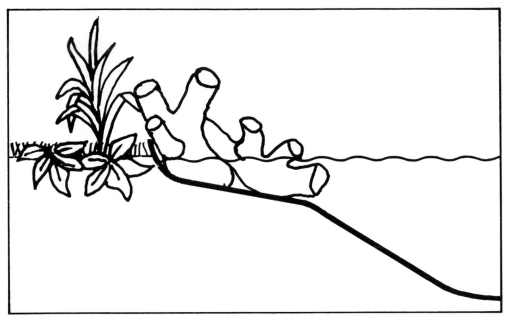

*Above: To avoid polluting the water, use only completely sound pieces of wood to landscape the marsh zone.*

*Below: To soften, the visual transition from its surroundings to the pond proper, place large rocks both inside and immediately outside the edge of the liner.*

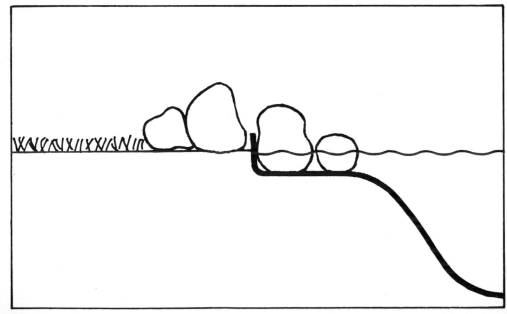

*Above and opposite page: A well-chosen, thoughtfully laid-out selection of marginal plants contributes enormously to the visual appeal of a water garden.*

zontal shelf or pan-shaped hollow with a depth of some 4″-12″ (10–30 cm) has to be provided around the margin of the pond. The advantages of this design are that it can be used for smaller ponds, the materials used make for a very decorative effect and the area offers a splendid refuge for amphibians and aquatic invertebrates.

A useful planting tip: to easily and successfully set out plants between pieces of wood or stones that are very close together, take a piece of ladies' stocking, tie it at the bottom and fill it up with soil. Then set the plant in the soil filled stocking, which is then positioned between the decorations in a manner that assures the earth will be kept constantly moist.

Once planting and the layout of the edge zone are completed, an overflow can be built if required.

Remember, its coupling must be fitted stress-free. Start by cutting a round hole into the liner, then screw the coupling into place. If necessary, firm up the liner's backing with sand. Finally, fit into place the connecting piece, a tube or hose that projects a couple of inches above the desired water line.

## Filling the Pond and Fixing the Liner Edges

The pond is now ready to be filled. As it is easier to emplace trays or tubs in the deep water zone before the pond is filled, this is a good time to set out water lilies or any other plants intended for this end of the pond. Apart from the greater ease of positioning such containers in a dry basin, there is less likelihood of disturbing their dressing of gravel if the water level is slowly raised to cover them. This minimizes the risk that soil will be stirred up, with the inevitable increase in turbidity and loss of visibility. It is also much simpler to plant the marsh zone before it is inundated if the plants are to be grown directly in a layer of soil. However, the risk of muddying the water is considerably less if the decision is made to set out the marsh plants in containers after the pond is completely filled. Once the marsh zone has been planted, the water level can be raised to its maximum level. This assures that the roots of these plants will remain damp.

Now that the pond is filled and planted, it should be left to settle down for a week. During this period, the weight of the water will have compacted the bed and the liner should have settled down flat everywhere within the basin. Once this initial settling is completed, it is possible to determine the final water level. The coupling for any intended overflow drain will also have settled in position so the hose leading to the sump or the surface drainage channel can also be loosely laid in or on a bed of sand.

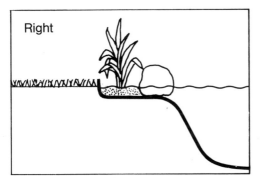
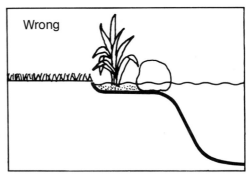

*The liner should not be cut too short in order to prevent water from flowing into the soil.*

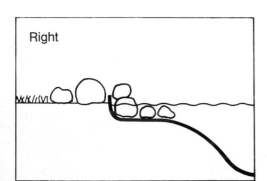
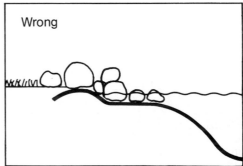

*The end of the liner should be drawn between rocks in order to keep the water in the pond.*

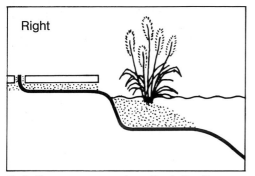

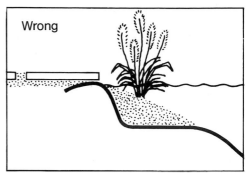

*Only the arrangement on the left will assure a watertight pond.*

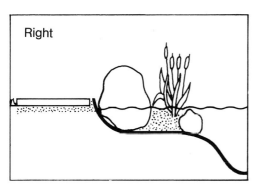

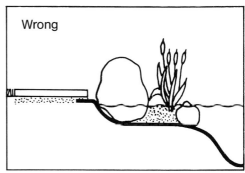

*If the liner is not property set (right), a heavy rock placed near the pond margin will force it down and allow water to overflow into the surrounding yard.*

## How to Stabilize and Seal the Edges of the Pond

If at any point the water and the surrounding soil came into contact, water will be drawn out of the pond by capillary action. This is usually noticed after the water level has fallen excessively while the areas surrounding the pond are seen to be wet. It is easy to effect a perfect seal if the pond liner is used as the required barrier between soil and water. Sadly, there is one mistake all too frequently committed by novice pond builders. Namely, once the pond has been made, they cut off the surplus liner too hastily and, more importantly, too closely. If the soil only gives way a little under the weight of the boulders or other decorative materials in the margin

and marsh zones, the water will run out of the pond under the edging.

It is essential to remember that the completed pond will contain several tons of water pressing against the bottom and side walls. Rocks can depress the soil they are resting on and further pull in the edges of the liner. Plants that progagate vegetatively by runners further press down on the liner and scramble onto the margins of the pond. All these factors bring about changes in soil stability that can cause minor earth movements over the course of the following winter. Only after these have occurred might it be noticed that the allowance originally made for "shrinkage" in the liner was insufficient. Efforts to correct such an error of judgement at a later date are expensive. Thus always leave a safety margin of c. 1″–1¼″ (2–3 cm) when judging where to cut off the liner — at least until the first winter has passed. The final, definitive fixing of the liner edges must be undertaken very carefully and only after an appropriate measure of forethought.

The liner must be positioned so as to form a barrier between the water and the surrounding area, as described in pages 56–57. Long term settling of the liner can draw its edges inwards. This can allow the surrounding soil to come into contact with the water. At no point along the perimeter of the pond can capillary forces be allowed to start drawing water out of the basin. For this reason, it is unwise to be hasty about trimming the liner to its final dimensions. Leave at least 1″–1½″ (2–3 cm) more liner than estimated in place for at least one winter. By this time, the pond should have settled to its greatest degree, making it safe to trim any excess length from the liner.

# General Pond Maintenance

## The Water

The first factor to consider in any discussion of pond maintenance is water quality. Tap water is perfectly acceptable for pond use. Since most gardens have a ready source of water, filling the pond entails no more than connecting a hose to the nearest faucet and turning the tap. It is not a good idea to use either collected rainwater or stream water to fill the pond. The former is usually the accumulated run-off from the roofs of houses or garages. This means all the harmful substances deposited thereupon during a short dry spell or, worse still, brought there by brief showers, are put into the pond. Even waiting until an extended period of rainfall has cleaned both air and roofs of particulate matter does not always guarantee a usable water supply in all parts of North America. Acid precipitation is a serious and growing problem in the Canadian Maritime Provinces and the northeastern United States.

Rain collected in these areas is likely to be far too acidic for pond use.

Streams are an unreliable source of water for the garden pond. If the watershed lies in an area of intensive agriculture, stream water may contain high concentrations of dissolved fertilizers. Filling a pond with such water is an invitation for suspended algae to multiply explosively, creating a problem that is much more easily prevented than solved. Streams may also contain dissolved industrial wastes that can prove very toxic to fish in a closed system like the garden pond. All things considered, tap water represents the safest as well as the most convenient alternative to filling a pond.

It is best to allow the newly filled pond to sit a few days before introducing the first fish. This allows any chlorine present to dissipate and gives the incipient flora of nitrifying bacteria sufficient time to dispose of chloramine should this product be present in the municipal water supply. Slight turbidity caused by the suspension of soil particles during the filling process is normal. It should disappear within a few days. A light bloom of suspended algae, giving the water a greenish tinge, is also perfectly normal right after a pond has been filled. It should also quickly disappear once the vascular plants present in the pond begin to grow actively and in the process outcompete the algae for available nutrients. Within a week to ten days, the pond water will be clear and have a pleasant, fresh "natural" odor. At this point, fish can be safely added to the pond.

As already noted, sun and wind will cause water to evaporate. In most parts of North America, rainfall quickly refills the pond. In regions characterized by frequent summer rainfall, it is necessary to top up the water level only after protracted dry spells. In the southwestern United States, on the other hand, topping up the pond can be a weekly task during the summer months. Fluctuations of up to 2½″ (c. 6.0 cm) in the water level harm neither plants nor aquatic animals. It is unnecessary to treat such relatively small volumes of fresh water with dechlorinating agents. Dechlorination or dechloramination is prudent if more than a third of the pond's volume is replaced at any one time.

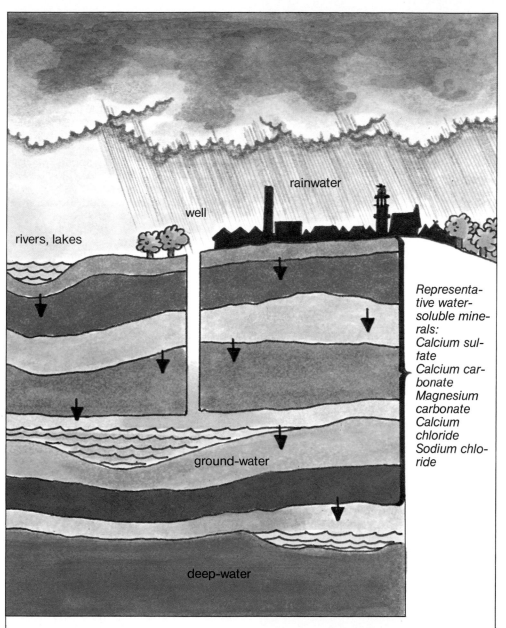

rainwater

well

rivers, lakes

Representative water-soluble minerals:
Calcium sulfate
Calcium carbonate
Magnesium carbonate
Calcium chloride
Sodium chloride

ground-water

deep-water

*As it trickles through the ground, rain water picks up a substantial burden of dissolved substances.*

## To Filter or Not . . .

Under ideal circumstances, filtration is not necessary for the garden pond. This is particularly true for large, well-planted ponds lightly stocked with fish whose foraging behavior does not disturb the planting medium or otherwise stir up bottom sediments. If these conditions do not obtain in his system, the pondkeeper may well find it necessary to fall back upon some type of filtration to promote water clarity and assure the well-being of his fish.

A pond filter is recommended should any of the following circumstances obtain:

— If the ratio of shallow to deep water works out to the detriment of the latter. This can result in rapid overheating of the pond, resulting in oxygen deficiency.

— if the pond is situated in a region where summer temperatures in excess of 80°F (c. 25°C) are routinely recorded for periods of three days or longer. Overheating is also a problem under these circumstances for all but the largest ponds.

— if there is a sharp temperature gradient between the water zones, i.e. as in a small pond whose sides fall away steeply.

— if the pond contains too few actively growing vascular plants to inhibit the growth of suspended algae.

— if the pond houses fish that forage actively in the substrate, thus stirring up debris and soil particles.

— if the pond is heavily stocked with fish

The last three contingencies are particularly likely to occur if colored carp are the intended residents of a pond.

The simplest and most economical approach to pond filtration entails the use of an air-driven sponge filter such as Tetra's Brillant G powered by a high capacity outdoor pump such as Tetra's Luft Pump 500. Such an arrangement both filters and aerates the pond water. The filter itself is

*Small heavily stocked ponds such as these are the most likely beneficiaries of some sort of filtration system.*

*TetraPond Brillant Filter.*

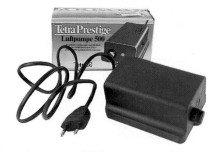

*Tetra Luftpump 500.*

*No pond filter can restore water clarity to a pond as heavily stocked as this. Adding floating plants such as water hyacinth may cut down on the algal bloom somewhat, but only reducing the number of fish present will completely eliminate this problem.*

easily cleaned, a task best performed every three or four weeks under normal circumstances. Such units are ideal for use in planted ponds, as they do not produce sufficient water movement to seriously inhibit the growth of water lilies.

Colored carp fanciers often find that more drastic expedients are necessary to maintain both visibility and water quality in their ponds. High capacity motor driven pond filters are available from water plant suppliers. If such a unit fails to produce satisfactory conditions, the only alternative is to consult with a nursery man or landscape architect on the design of a power-driven sand bed filter.

Regardless of type, filters require regular maintenance to perform effectively. Their task is simplified if the pondkeeper makes a practice of removing dead leaves and flower stalks from aquatic plants as soon as they are noticed. Overfeeding causes as many problems in the garden pond as in an aquarium. Many seemingly intractable water quality problems disappear dramatically when restraint is exercised at feeding time.

# Planting the Garden Pond

## Basic Principles of Water Gardening

Growing aquatic and bog plants is perhaps one of the easiest as well as most aesthetically satisfying forms of gardening. Compared to many other ornamental plants, they are hardy, undemanding and gratifyingly pest-free. However, to succeed as a water gardener, it is necessary to understand and apply a few basic principles. Once these have been explained, the prospective pond-keeper can then intelligently choose which of the many desirable candidates he plans on cultivating in his backyard pool.

## Planting Containers Vs. Natural Beds

With the exception of floating plants such as duckweed, aquatic and bog plants require a solid substrate in which to establish their roots. The traditional approach to satisfying this need has been to spread a layer of soil 6″ to 12″ (c. 15.0 cm–30.0 cm) deep over the bottom of the pond before it is filled. The desired plants are set out while the pond is still empty, then a layer of fine gravel or coarse sand 1″ (c. 2.5 cm) deep is spread over the surface of the planting medium. Finally, the pond is slowly filled and nature allowed to take its course.

However simple it might appear to implement, this natural bed approach to planting has serious shortcomings. Because it exposes such a large surface to contact with the water, this approach encourages eutrophication and the algal "blooms" consequent upon it even when the medium in question is nutrient poor. A thick layer of soil over the entire bottom increases the risk that trapped pockets of organic matter will undergo anaerobic decay due to poor water circulation within the planting medium. This can result in the uncontrolled release of toxic hydrogen suplhide gas, with devastating consequences for any fish present. Finally, it greatly complicates the task of maintaining water clarity. Even with a gravel dressing, it is impossible to prevent bottom foraging fish such as goldfish and colored carp from stirring up the medium sufficiently to suspend fine soil particles.

These problems can be avoided if water lilies, lotus or other submerged plants are set out in individual planting containers rather than an extensive bed of planting medium spread out over the bottom of the deep water zone. As the total area exposed

to the water is quite small, such containers of planting medium release fewer dissolved nutrients into the pond water. Their modest surface area affords fewer opportunities for bottom-foraging fish to roil their contents, which in any event can be protected by a deeper dressing of gravel if necessary.

Finally, the depth at which such containers rest is easily regulated by the expeditious use of cinder blocks or bricks to lift them off the bottom. This makes it possible to control the single most important variable in water gardening, the amount of light reaching the submerged plant, with considerable precision. Such flexibility is of great advantage in the culture of many aquatic plants, particu-

*Marsh plants such as these naturalize most effectively if planted in an open bed rather than in containers.*

larly in ponds that do not enjoy full sunlight throughout the day.

The advantages of container planting are less striking in the marsh zone. The natural bed approach is unlikely to contribute significantly to eutrophication if applied here, and certainly cannot cause increased turbidity. Obviously, if the object is to encourage naturalization of such bog plants as marsh marigolds or iris, they are best planted in such a bed. The chief advantages of containerized planting apply to the cultivation of subjects that are not reliably winter hardy. Such plants suffer far less trauma when moved indoors if they are already growing in a pot or planting tray.

## Types of Planting Containers

The redwood or cedar planting tubs formerly recommended as receptacles for aquatic plants are still to be found in nurseries, but these bulky — and expensive —

containers have been largely displaced by plastic tubs, pans and trays. A visit to any hardware store or home supply center will reveal a wide selection of suitable containers for use in the garden pond. Lotus, some of the more robust hardly water lilies, and elephant ear require planting tubs of 20 to 30 quart capacity (c. 22–35 l). The majority of hardy lilies and other submerged plants prosper if planted in pans of 11 quart to 14 quart (c. 12–15 l) capacity. Tropical lilies seem to prefer more water circulation about their roots than their hardy relatives. Special planting baskets with mesh liners designed to satisfy this requirement are available from aquatic nurseries at modest prices. For obvious aesthetic reasons, choose only dark-colored plastic containers for pond use. Both plastic and clay flower pots make excellent containers for both aquatic and bog plants. As these plants tend to be shallow rooted, bulb pans are often better suited for their culture than standard flower pots.

## Planting Media

Most aquatic and bog plants are shallow rooters that depend to a considerable degree upon direct absorption of dissolved nutrients via their stems and leaves for normal growth. This is particularly true of submerged aquatic plants like *Anacharis* or *Cabomba*. Consequently, these plants do not need a nutrient-rich planting medium to flourish. As a rule, nutrient inflow from the breakdown of organic matter that falls into the pond and of the excreta of fish and other pond inhabitants will make up any deficiencies in this regard.

Aquatic plants potted in compost, humus or topsoil richly endowed with organic matter will certainly grow luxuriantly. However, excess nutrients that leak into solution from such media lead to the eutrophication of the garden pond. This state of affairs arises from an oversupply of plant nutrients in solution that favours the growth of algae at the expense of vascular plants. Such spectacular "blooms" of both suspended and attached algae will recur yearly until the reservoir of nutrients available in the planting medium is exhausted. The resulting loss of water clarity can completely ruin any enjoyment of a pond for years to come.

For most bog and aquatic plants, a mixture of equal parts poor garden soil and gravel with a particle size range of ¼″–1¼″ (c. 0.5–3.0 cm) suffices to meet their nutritional

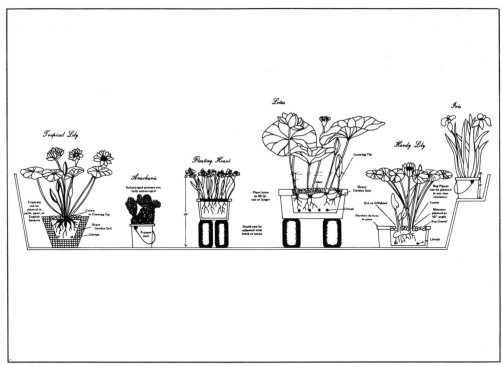

*Planting diagram from Lilypons Catalogue.*

needs. The spoil from the excavation of the pond basin is usually an acceptable source of soil for the planting medium. Water lilies, lotus and some tropical bog plants require a heavier medium to prosper. A mixture of three parts clay-rich subsoil to one part of gravel satisfies their needs during their initial period of growth. Special fertilizer tablets are available from aquatic nurseries, should supplementary feeding during the growing season be required. Relatively low in nitrogen but high in phosporus and potash, these tablets will not ignite an algal bloom if used according to instructions. Between 10" and 12" (c. 25.0 cm–30.0 cm) of planting medium are required to accommodate the robust root systems of water lilies, lotus and some of the larger tropical bog plants. The majority of aquatic and bog plants will root and grow satisfactorily in 4"– 8" (c. 10.0–20.0 cm) of planting medium. When selecting a planting container, bear in mind that it must be deep enough to accom-modate both the planting medium and about 1" (c. 2.5 cm) of coarse sand or fine gravel top dressing. The generous use of such an inert "cap" is strongly recommend-ed to minimize the tendency of fine soil par-ticles to go into suspension. Such turbidity is most unsightly and more easily prevented than corrected.

**Planting Techniques**
Bog plants should be set out in the same manner as other ornamental plants in the "dry" garden. The use of commercially avail-able vitamin B solutions to minimze trans-planting shock is equally applicable to them. Bear in mind when spacing bog plants that most species grow very rapidly and manifest a tendency to spread well beyond their initial foothold. A degree of moderation when setting out the marsh zone's planting is thus strongly recom-mended.

The accompanying diagram illustrates how to plant aquatic subjects such as lilies, lotus, and bunch plants. The usual problem encountered with aquatic species is holding them down long enough for them to set roots. A rock of appropriate dimensions placed atop the rootstalks of lilies and lotus usually suffices to keep them in place after planting. The lead strips sold to hold the cuttings of bunch plants in place under aquarium conditions work equally well in the garden pond. It is equally important to resist the temptation to overplant the pond proper. Water lilies require from 3 to 12 square feet (c. 1 to 4 m²) of pond surface per plant to prosper. Lotus are even more demanding. A single flourishing specimen of either plant makes a far showier display than three or four overcrowded stragglers.

The marsh zone can be planted at any time. However, it is much easier to set out aquatic plants **before** the pond is filled. Supporting blocks for lily or lotus tubs are more easily positioned in the deep zone while the basin is still empty. The same holds for pans or trays destined for the transitional zone. There is also less likelihood of disturbing the planting medium or dislodging the plants themselves if the water level rises slowly around the planting containers.

It is not a good idea to collect wild marsh or aquatic plants for use in the garden pond. Many species are protected by law against such exploitation. Those that are not often prove to be the vectors of plant pests such as the "sandwich man", an aquatic caterpillar that can devastate the leaves of water lilies or other floating plants, or of fish parasites. It is always best to purchase cultivated, pest and disease-free plants from a commercial establishment such as a water garden, nursery or tropical fish retailer.

When laying out the garden pond, aim for a planting scheme that assures some plants will be in flower throughout the growing season. As many bog plants are among the earliest of spring bloomers and a fair number will flower through the first frost, it is possible to enjoy a water garden virtually from the spring thaw to autumn leaf fall. Few other gardens offer so much pleasure for so little effort.

*Plants in a garden pond must be planted in a suitable depth of water. This partially drained pond shows the shallow water marginals around the edge and the deeper water plants in the middle.*

### Pests and Enemies of Water Plants

Compared to their terrestrial counterparts, aquatic and bog plants have relatively few insect pests. Several species of aphids will attack water lilies and lotus, as well as the more succulent leafed bog plants. As chemical insecticides are extremely toxic to fish, this approach to their control is not applicable to water gardening. The best approach entails using a high-pressure spray of water to wash the aphids into the water, where they undergo an instantaneous change in status from plant pest to fish food!

The potential of the larvae of the delta moth to damage the foliage of floating plants has already been noted. Fortunately, this pest can be controlled by biological means that pose no risk to pond fish. It is susceptible to attack by *Bacillus thuringiensis,* a bacterium widely used as a means of controlling lawn and garden pests. Such products as

Dipel HG are based on dormant cultures of this bacterium. Used according to the manufacturer's instructions, they provide a safe and effective control of aquatic lepidopteran larvae.

Ducks, turtles and crayfish all feed on aquatic plants. The first two are unlikely to visit, much less establish themselves in a garden pond unless put there by the pondkeeper himself. Many crayfish, to the contrary, are quite capable of overland movement. Suburban water gardeners whose yards lie near a stream or lake can often find themselves hosting these unwelcome guests. Crayfish succumb to chemical insecticides, but so do fish. Thus the only safe way to be rid of them is to trap them out. Crayfish will enter commercially available

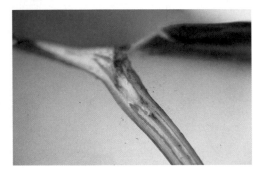

*(Above) Larva of **Murvessa gyralis,** another harmful aquatic moth, burrowing in a water stem.*
*(Below) Adults of three common months whose aquatic larvae can damage water lilies. In all instances, female left, male right. Top, **Poraponyx obsuralis,** center, **Munroessa gyralis,** bottom, **Eoparargyractis irroratalis.***

minnow traps baited with a piece of meat or fish. Set the baited trap out in the evening and check for results the next morning. A swift stamp of a shod foot suffices to dispose of any crayfish present. Crayfish are delicious when prepared in the same manner as shrimp or lobster, but hopefully the pondkeeper will never be so troubled by them as to make this approach to disposing of them practical!

# Plants for the Garden Pond

### Introduction
A pleasingly landscaped garden pond must draw upon three groups of plants: bog plants, large-flowered aquatic plants such as water lilies and lotus, and a large selection of true aquatic plants of diverse growth habits. Each group is herein considered separately from the standpoint of general growing requirements and a selection of easily grown, generally available species given, together with relevant information on their culture. The following key will explain the coding employed to convey such information:

| Characteristic | Coding | |
|---|---|---|
| growth habit | U | – upright |
| | B | – bushy |
| | R | – recumbent |
| | N | – floating leaves |
| | S | – fully submerged |
| light requirements | S | – full sun (5 hrs./day) |
| | PS | – partial sun (3–5 hrs./day) |
| | S̶ | – filtered sunlight |
| fragrance | F | – flowers fragrant |
| | F̶ | – flowers without scent |
| water depth over crown of plant | D | – followed by values |

Because winter conditions vary greatly from south to north, plants that are reliably winter hardy in one area may not overwinter successfully outdoors in another. The same holds true of fish. The accompanying map shows the agro-climate zonation scheme developed by the U. S. Department of Agriculture and adopted by farmers and nurserymen throughout North America. A plant that is handy from Zone 10–Zone 6 can be left outside over the winter in the corresponding regions laid out on the map. Another way of phrasing the same point is to refer to a plant as hardy to Zone 6. North of this map zone, the plant in question must either be overwintered indoors or grown as an annual. This system of describing winter hardiness is employed throughout the remainder of this book. Bear in mind that many bog and aquatic plants can be grown very successfully as annuals north of their critical range limits for winter hardiness. Hence the fact that they will not survive the winter should not deter the pondkeeper from attempting their culture.

## Bog Plants

This diverse group of subjects shares one feature in common: they live with their feet in the water but their heads in the air! Hence they are candidates for the marsh zone, or less commonly, the marginal or transitional zone of the garden pond. They can be operationally divided into three subdivisions: vertical accent plants, flowering plants and ornamental foliage plants. Each group has its place in a well laid-out water garden.

## Vertical Accent Plants

This group consists of the sedges, rushes and cattails. Their flowers are generaly inconspicuous and their foliage unadorned. Their chief contribution to the decor of a garden pond is to set it off from the remainder of the garden and provide a suitable backdrop for the pond proper and the other plants associated with it. These plants are easily grown and have a tendency to spread *very* rapidly once established, both vegetatively and by seed. It is thus a good idea to restrict them to a planting container or, if they are planted in a natural bed, limit their potential lateral spread with metal or plastic barrier strips. Seed heads can be snipped off after the first frost to preclude their dispersal.

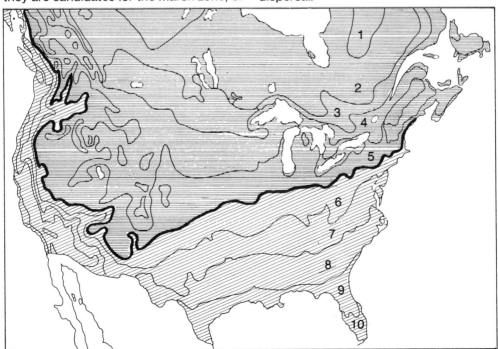

*Refer to this agro-climatic zone map to determine the winter-hardiness of the ornamental plants discussed in the text in a given area.*

Cattail *(Typha latifolia);* Narrow-leafed Cattail *(T. angustifolia):* U to 7′ (c. 2.3 m); FS/PS; D to 12″ (c. 30 cm); Zones 2–10; distinctive inflorescence and seed heads produced August to October; ***extremely invasive;*** recommended for large ponds only.

Spike Rush *(Eleocharis montevidensis):* U to 12″ (c. 30 cm); FS/PS; D to 12″ (c. 30 cm); Zones 6–0; has distinctive club-like seed pod; recommended for small ponds.

Dwarf Cattail *(Typha minima):* U to 4′ (c. 1.2 m); FS:PS; D to 12″ (c. 30 cm); Zones 3–10; ***extremely invasive;*** suitable for small ponds.
Sweet Flag *(Acorus calamus):* U to 30″ (c. 90 cm); FS/PS; D to 6″ (c. 15 cm); Zones 4–10; leaves have strong, sweet aroma when crushed.

Umbrella Palm *(Cyperus alternifolius):* U to 5′ (c. 1–6 m); FS/PS; D to 6″ (c. 15 cm); Zones 9–10; does not grow as tall when planted in a container; ***very invasive*** where winter hardy.
Dwarf Papyrus *(Cyperus haspans);* U to 30″ (c. 90 cm); FS/PS; D to 6″ (c. 15 cm); Zones 9–10.
Dwarf Cyperus *(Cyperus sp.):* U to 18″ (c. 45 cm); FS/PS; D to 6″ (c. 15 cm); Zones 9–10; recommended for small ponds.

*Opposite: Vertical accent plants have been used to set this pond off from the remainder of the garden while providing a pleasant background for indoor viewers or from the adjoining patio.*

*Both Siberian (upper right) and yellow water iris (lower left) naturalize readily in all save the coldest parts of North America. Large clumps such as these make a glorious late spring display in the water garden.*

## Flowering Plants

The showy blossoms of these plants earn them a place in the water garden. It is usually desirable to allow winter hardy species to naturalize freely. Hence the advantage of planting them in a natural bed. Where circumstances preclude this approach, they can be grown successfully in containers. With a few exceptions, to be duly noted, these plants are best treated as annuals north of their critical range limit.

Canna *(Canna* var.): U to 4' (c. 1.2 m) for standard varieties; 18" (c. 45 cm) for dwarf varieties; FS; D to 4" (c. 10 cm); Zones 7–10; large, showy flowers in colors from yellow and pink to dark red; many varieties have reddish bronze foliage; dwarf varieties best used in smaller ponds.

Peace Lily *(Spathiphyllum floribundum):* B to 15" (c. 37 cm); PS; D to 3" (c. 7.5 cm); Zone 10; overwinters well indoors.

Yellow Water Iris *(Iris pseudoacorus):* U to 30" (c. 90 cm); FS; F; D to 10" (c. 25 cm); Zones 4–9; early spring bloomer.

Red Iris *(Iris fulva):* U to 24" (c. 60 cm); FS; F; D to 6" (c. 15 cm); Zones 5–9; blooms early through late spring.

Blue Iris *(Iris versicolor):* U to 30" (c. 90 cm); FS; D to 6"; Zones 4–9; blooms early to mid-spring.

Siberian Iris *(Iris siberica):* U to 30" (c. 90 cm); FS; F; D to 4" (c. 10 cm); Zones 4–9; blossoms mid to late spring.

Arrowhead *(Sagittaria latifolia):* U to 24" (c. 60 cm); FS/PS; D to 6" (c. 15 cm); Zones 5–10; double-flowered varieties available.

Pickerel Rush *(Pontederia cordata):* U to 30" (c. 90 cm); FS:PS; D to 12" (c. 30 cm); Zones 3–9; blue and white flowered varieties available, very hardy.

Water Arum *(Peltandra virginica):* B to 24" (c. 60 cm); FS/PS; D to 6" (c. 15 cm); Zones 5–9; yellow green, calla lily-like flowers produced all summer long.

White Arum *(Peltandra sagittfolia):* B to 18" (c. 45 cm); FS; D to 6" (c. 15 cm); Zones 6–10; recommended for small ponds.

Bog Lily *(Crinum americanum):* U to 24" (c. 60 cm); FS/PS; F; D to 6" (c. 15 cm); Zones 8–10; large white flowers produced all summer long.

Marsh Marigold *(Caltha palustris):* B to 12″ (c. 30 cm); FS/PS; D to 4″ (c. 10 cm); Zones 2–5; brilliant yellow flowers in early spring; does not tolerate summer temperatures well south of Zone 5; naturalizes freely.

Lizards' tail *(Saururus cernuus):* B to 18″ (c. 45 cm); FS/PS; F; D to 6″ (c. 15 cm); Zones 4–9.

## Ornamental Foliage Plants
Though many of these plants flower freely, they are grown chiefly for their distinctive foliage. Unless specifically noted, these plants do not overwinter well indoors and are best grown as annuals north of their critical range limits.

Red Ludwigia *(Ludwigia natans):* R to 18″ (c. 45 cm); FS/PS; D to 12″ (c. 30 cm); Zones 8–10; along with the preceding species can be overwintered indoors in brightly lit aquaria; red leaf pigments fade under aquarium conditions.

Pennywort *(Hydrocotyle vulgaris):* R to 18″ (c. 45 cm); FS; D to 12″ (c. 30 cm); Zones 8–10; can be overwintered indoors in a brightly lit aquarium.

Taro *(Colocasia esculenta):* B to 40″ (c. 1.3 m); FS:PS; D to 8″ (c. 20 cm); Zones 9–10; also known as Elephant Ear; a violet stemmed, darker green variety is also available.

Parrot's feather *(Myriophyllum aquaticum):* R, N to 3′ (c. 1 m); FS/PS; D to 12″ (c. 30 cm); Zones 6–10; best planted in the transitional zone.

Sagittaria *(Sagittaria* spp.): U to 24″ (c. 60 cm); FS; D to 12″ (c. 60 cm); Zones 5–10.

Radicans swordplant *(Echinodorus cordifolius):* B to 30″ (c. 90 cm); FS/PS; D to 12″ (c. 30 cm); Zones 8–10; can be overwintered indoors under aquarium conditions.

Purple waffle plant *(Hemigraphis colorata):* B to 12″ (c. 30 cm); FS/PS; D to 10″ (c. 25 cm); Zones 9–10; will overwinter indoors as a terrarium or houseplant.

African Crypt *(Anubias lanceolata):* B to 12″ (c. 30 cm); PS; D to 12″ (c. 30 cm); Zone 10; can be overwintered under aquarium conditions indoors.

Scarlet Altenanthera *(Altenanthera reinekkii):* R to 18″ (c. 45 cm); FS/PS; D to 12″ (c. 30 cm); Zones 9–10.

## Water Lilies and Lotus

These are the true aristocrats of the water garden. It is rightly said that no pond is complete without a water lily. Given the remarkable selection available to choose from, it is equally safe to say that there is a water lily for every pond! Lotus are as undemanding as their distant relatives of the genus *Nymphae* and in many respects, their spectacular foliage and blossoms, held well above the water surface, make an even more spectacular display.

Water lilies are divided into two broad categories by aquatic gardeners. *Hardy lilies,* as their name implies, can survive the winter outdoors northward to Zone 3. They grow from a long rhizome and produce flowers that rest directly upon or are barely elevated above the water surface. All hardy lilies are day bloomers. Both lightly scented and scentless varieties are available in a rage of colors from white and yellow through pink and dark red.

All water lilies should have between 12″–18″ (30–45 cm) of water above their crowns. None relishes strong water movement or splashing of water onto their leaves. Hardy water lilies otherwise require minimum maintenance. Old leaves and spent flower heads should be removed as they appear. Heavy bloomers should also be fertilized monthly using the commercially formulated tablets discussed earlier. These lilies propagate vegatively by means of "eyes" that develop along the growing rhizome. It is usually necessary to divide and replant them every few years to assure optimum flower production. To prepare hardy lilies for the winter stop fertilizing with the advent of the first light frost. After the first heavy frost, prune away all the dead leaves and stems and if appropriate, place the planting container directly on the pond bottom at its deepest point. If the depth of the pond is insufficient to preclude freezing, move the container into a cool corner of the cellar and keep the planting medium barely moist until spring.

*Tropical water lilies* are not reliably winter hardy north of Zone 10, and even here require some protection against the occassional severe frost. They grow from a rounded tuber and produce flowers that are held well above the surface of the water. Both day and night blooming varieties are available. Day bloomers open their flowers in the morning and close them in the late afternoon. Night bloomers open at dusk and close at sunrise. Both scented and scentless day bloomers are available. All night blooming lilies are scented and many varieties are among the most bewitchingly fragrant of all ornamental plants. Day blooming tropicals range in flower color from white and yellow through pink and salmon to blue and a deep violet. Night bloomers come in rose red, pink and white. Many tropical lilies have handsome speckled bronze or maroon leaves. Some varieties are also *viviparous,* small plants appearing at the juncture of the leaf blade and stem as the growing season progresses.

Tropical water lilies require the same care during the growing season as their hardy cousins. Because their tubers are not easily stored over the winter and must in any event be induced to sprout in a heated aquarium before they can be set out once more in the pond, most water gardeners choose to grow them as annuals north of Zone 10. Viviparous tropicals are a partial exception to this generalization. If the plantlets are potted up well beforehand, they can usually be expected to survive satisfactorily in a well lit aquarium with other tropical aquatic plants. Water gardeners in Zone 10 must stay alert to frost warnings and be prepared to cover their ponds with sheet plastic to protect their tropical lilies.

The following water lilies are well suited to the garden pond. They are hardy, colorful and readily available. The varieties are arranged by flower color. The following conventions have been adopted to convey the most information possible in a limited space:

| Characteristic | Coding | |
|---|---|---|
| Type | H | – hardy |
| | T | – tropical |
| Blooming time | D | – day bloomer |
| | N | – night bloomer |
| Leaf spread | A | – 1'–6' (c. 30 cm$^2$–2 m$^2$) |
| | B | – 6'–12' (c. 2 m$^2$–4 m$^2$) |
| | C | – > 12' (> 4 m$^2$) |
| Foliage color | G | – green |
| | MT | – mottled |
| | BR | – bronze |
| | MN | – maroon |

### White

Marliac Albida: H; B; G; FS; F; prolific bloomer; good for small ponds.
Tuberosa: H; A/B; G; FS; good for small ponds.
Marian Strawn: T; D; A/B; MT; FS/PS; F
White Knight: T; N; B/C; G; FS/PS; F; very prolific bloomer.
Juno: T; N; B/C; G; FS/PS; F; container can be placed up to 3' (c. 1m) deep with good results.

### Yellow

Chromatella: H; A/B; MT; FS/PS; very long blooming season; excellent for small ponds.
Helvola: H; A; MT; FS/PS; a true pygmy lily, with flowers the size of a 50 cent piece; excellent for small ponds.
Suphurea: H; A/B; MT; FS/PS; holds flowers just above surface, excellent for small ponds.
Yellow Dazzler: T; D; B; MT; FS; F; flowers remain open until dusk.

### Changeable

Graziella: H; A; MT; FS/PS; flower yellow upon opening changing to rosy orange; excellent for small ponds.
Paul Hariot: H; A; MT; FS/PS; flower rosy yellow upon opening changing to pink; excellent for small ponds.
Golden West: T; D; B; MN; FS/PS; F; flower salmon pink on opening, changing to apricot.

*Yellow Dazzler (top), Paul Hariot (center), Texas Shell Pink (bottom).*

*Graziella (top), Fabiola (center), Froebeli (bottom).*

79

*Purpurata (top), Dauben (center), American Lotus "Lutea" (bottom).*

*Maroon Beauty (top), Panama Pacific (center), Asiatic Lotus "Miniature", "Momo Botan" (bottom).*

### Pink

Fabiola: H; A/B; G; FS; often produces several flowers at a time.

Joanne Pring: H; A; G; FS; excellent for small ponds.

Texas Shell Pink: T; N; B/C; G; FS/PS; F; prolific bloomer.

### Red

Ellisiana: H; A/B; G; FS; excellent for small ponds.

Froebeli: H; A; G; FS; very dark red flowers; excellent for small ponds.

Purpurata: H; A; G; FS; excellent for small ponds; withstands high summer temperatures better than preceding two varieties.

Emily G. Hutchings: T; N; B/C; BR; FS/PS; F; often produces flowers in clusters.

Maroon Beauty: T; N; B/C; MN; FS; F.

### Blue and Purple

Colorata: T; D; A; G; FS/PS; F; a true pigmy lily that will grow in as little as 6" (c. 15 cm) of water; excellent for small ponds.

Dauben: T; D; A/B; MT; FS/PS; F; best lily for low light areas; highly viviparous; excellent for small ponds.

Mrs. Martin E. Randig: T; D; A/C; G; FS/PS; F; adapts equally well to large and small ponds; highly viviparous.

Robert Strawn: T; D; A/B; MT; FS/PS; F; lavender flowers held well above the surface.

Panama Pacific: T; D; A/C; MT; FS/PS; F; deep purple flowers; highly viviparous; adapts equally well to large and small ponds.

Lotus differ from water lilies in their emergent growth pattern. All *Nelumbo* species hold both leaves and blooms well clear of the water surface. This makes them particularly valuable in landscaping ponds intended to house colored carp, whose herbivorous tendencies and need for filtration make life difficult for water lilies. Lotus are also more of an edge plant than *Nymphea*. They do not prosper if planted deeper than 1' (c. 30 cm) and flourish best with no more than 4"–6" (c. 10 cm–15 cm) of water over their crown. Their culture is otherwise identical to that of hardy lilies. Be certain to use only the largest available planting containers for lotus, as they proliferate much more rapidly under pond conditions than do lilies. Lotus do not do well under the subtropical conditions of Zone 10. Elsewhere, they are a hardy and undemanding asset to any water garden.

Because of their robust dimensions, only a few lotus are well suited to small to medium sized garden ponds. The native American species, *Nelumbo pentapetala,* is hardy through Zone 4. It is often sold under the varietal name Lutea with reference to its pale yellow flowers. Miniature Momo Botan is a dwarf dark red double flowered variety of the Asiatic lotus, *N. nucifera*. It will overwinter reliably through Zone 5.

### Submerged and Floating Aquatic Plants

These plants are often sold as "oxygenating plants". This is a misnomer, for while they release oxygen during the daylight hours as a by-product of photosynthesis, they are net oxygen consumers at night. This actually puts them in direct competition for available oxygen with the fish. The real contribution these plants make to the biological equilibrium of a pond is to serve as biological "sinks" for dissolved nutrients that would otherwise fuel unsightly algae blooms. Water hyacinth and water lettuce are particularly efficient competitors for available nutrients and can quickly "starve" an algal bloom out of existence.

This is not to deny the aesthetic contribution these plants make to a garden pond. Many have pleasing foliage or colorful flowers and are well worth cultivating for these alone. Fully submerged plants also provide spawning sites for many pond fish and refuge for fry or adults of timid species. They thus have an important role to play in the life of a garden pond.

These are easily grown plants that flourish in the nutrient-poor basic planting medium recommended for pond plants. Most rooted species do not usually prosper at depths in excess of 12" (c. 30 cm). Hence their containers should be set in the transitional zone or atop concrete blocks tall enough to bring them up to the appropriate depth in the deep water zone. Remember, when planting any of the species that grow from a central point that this crown must be **above** the surface of the substrate, a distinction that extends to the top dressing if this is employed in the container.

Many of the cold sensitive species considered herein will prosper in well-lit aquaria indoors. This is the simplest way to overwinter them successfully. The following list is by no means exhaustive. Many popular aquarium plants such as the numerous *Hygrophilla* and *Echinodorus* species do very well outside during the summer months. It never hurts to experiment in this manner. Success may even mean that the aquarist has the opportunity to see the emergent form and flowers of these old acquaintances for the first time.

A word of caution: do not introduce any of the duckweeds *(Lemna)* or floating ferns *(Salvinia, Azolla)* into the garden pond. They tend to multiply explosively and quickly become a first-rate nuisance, obscuring visibility, blocking off light to submerged plants and clogging filters and pump intakes. It is much easier to prevent such an infestation than eliminate it.

Anacharis *(Elodea canadensis):* S, B, to 3' (c. 1 cm); FS; D to 30" (c. 75 cm); Zones 5–10; prefers cooler water.

Cabomba *(Cabomba coroliniana):* S, B, to 15" (c. 37 cm); S; D to 24" (c. 60 cm); Zones 6–10; does best in cooler water. Ambulia *(Nemophila* sp.) is a very similar plant that tolerates warm water much better than Cabomba.

Vallisneria *(Vallisneria* spp.): S, U to 24" (c. 60 cm); S; D to 24" (c. 30 cm); available in a wide range of foliage types and sizes; *V. americana* will overwinter outside from Zone 4–10; varieties grown for aquarium use not reliably winter hardy north of Zone 9; spreads rapidly by means of runners.

Myriophyllum *(Myriophyllum* spp.): S, B to 24" (c. 60 cm); FS; D to 24" (c. 60 cm); Zones 4–10; an excellent spawning medium for egg scattering fish.

Hornwort *(Ceratophyllum demersum):* N, R to 3' (c. 1 cm); FS; Zones 5–10; aquarium cultivates not reliably hardy north of Zone 8; excellent refuge plant for fry.

Water Lettuce *(Pistia stratoides):* N; FS/PS; Zones 9–10; a fully floating plant whose elaborate root system provides an ideal spawning site for egg scattering fish; prohibited in Texas.

Floating Heart *(Nymphoides peltata):* N; FS/PS; D from 4"–12" (c. 10 cm–30 cm); Zones 6–10; fringed yellow flowers held well above the water; blooms from late spring to early fall; treat like a hardy water lily.

Water Poppy *(Hydrocleys nymphoides):* N; FS/PS; D from 4"–12" (c. 10 cm–30 cm); Zone 9–10; prohibited in California; bright yellow flowers held above the water; treat like a tropical water lily.

Water Hyacinth *(Eichornia crassipes):* N; FS; Zones 9–10; a showy, easily grown floating plant whose roots make an excellent spawning site for egg scatterers; both blue and white flowered varieties available; has become a serious navigational obstacle in subtropical and tropical areas where it has become naturalized; prohibited in Florida and Texas; shipment across state lines also prohibited in the U.S.; neither this nor the preceding species adapt well to indoor aquaria.

# Residents of the Garden Pond

## Introduction
The opportunity to cultivate colorful aquatic and bog plants is only half of a garden pond's appeal. The other derives from its ability to support numerous interesting and equally attractive animal residents, ranging from snails and dragon flies through fish and frogs. The aim of this section is to present a selection of ornamental fish that will prosper in an outdoor setting and to introduce some of the other creatures that can be expected to show up in an established pond as either full-time residents or casual visitors. Space limitations preclude detailed treatment of all of these groups. The interested reader is referred to the reference titles listed in the Suggested Readings section for additional information.

## Ornamental Fish
As their name implies, these fish are kept for the aesthetic satisfaction they afford. **Pond fish must thus appear attractive when seen from above.** This limits the number of suitable pool residents, for under natural conditions, predator pressure selects stringently against color patterns easily perceived from overhead. Thus many fish that show up well when viewed from the side in an aquarium effectively vanish from sight when placed in a pond setting. The role of predation also goes far towards explaining why many of the most popular pond fish are *catatechnic* or artifically selected color varieties whose persistance requires continuous human intervention.

Pond keepers throughout the world's temperate zones have the opportunity to enjoy the doyen of all ornamental pond fish, the goldfish, as well as their more robust cousins, the spectacular nishiki-goi, or colored carp. Hence the pride of place afforded these popular pool fish herein. European coldwater fish keepers have long appreciated the merits of many of their native species as pond residents. However, few of those species are available to North American pond enthusiasts. This is in large measure due to unease over the possibility of their accidental introduction and subsequent establishment in natural waters prevalent in official circles. It is thus unlikely the regulatory climate that precludes marketing such species of the tench *(Tinca tinca)* in many jurisdictions will alter in the foreseeable future.

Fortunately, North American pond keepers can draw on a much larger selection of colorful native fishes than can their European counterparts. A representative selection of desirable and generally available native pool fish is presented herein, along with a synopsis of relevant maintenance information. Finally, it is perfectly possible to summer most tropical aquarium fish successfully in an outdoor pond. The concluding section of this discussion of ornamental fishes outlines workable approaches and suggests which groups are most likely to prosper in such an environment.

## Stocking the Garden Pond
The novice pond keeper often makes the mistake of stocking his new pool's full complement of fish at a single throw. This frequently is followed by a series of "mysterious" deaths over a ten to fourteen day period which cease as abruptly as they began. The cause of these mortalities is inadvertant nitrogen cycle mismanagement. A pond, like an aquarium, must be given sufficient time to develop a mature bacterial flora capable of degrading nitrogenous fish wastes to harmless nitrate. This process takes somewhat longer to accomplish in an outdoor pond, where cooler temperatures slow bacterial growth significantly. It is thus best to add a new pond's residents one or two at a time at two or three day intervals over a three to four week "settling-in" period. The pond keeper who adopts this approach rarely has cause to complain of inexplicable losses of newly stocked fish.

The second tempation the novice must confront is that of overstocking. It is particularly difficult to resist if the fish in question are juvenile specimes, as is often the case with both goldfish and nishiki-goi. A pond, like an aquarium, has a finite carrying capacity. If that capacity is exceeded, losses are inevi-

table. It is easy to disregard this injunction early in the season, when low water temperatures depress the fishes' metabolic rates sufficiently to preclude either respiratory distress or nitrite intoxication. The moment of truth comes with the first heat wave. Then elevated water temperatures inexorably enforce every pond's inherent limit to sustain aquatic life.

Remember, too, when stocking fish that their growth under pond conditions is far more rapid than it would be in an aquarium. Four to six 3″ nishiki-goi may not seem to be like a lot of fish for a 5′ × 9′ pond when they are put out for the first time in mid-May, but they will fill the pond quite comfortably by the end of August! Other fish may not be able to match this sort of rapid growth, but they also can be expected to gain considerably in size by the end of the growing season. Hence the importance of stocking a pond conservatively at the onset. Unless otherwise noted, an inch (c. 2.5 cm) of fish per 7 gallons (c. 30 l) of pond capacity is a good rule to follow when stocking the garden pond.

**Overwintering Pond Fish**
Where a pond keeper lives determines how he will care for his fish during the winter months. In Zones 9 and 10, no special precautions need be taken to assure the survival of coldwater species, though lower win-

ter water temperatures should dictate restraint when feeding. Though outdoor fish remain active throughout the year in these regions, lower winter temperatures will depress their appetites.

Pond fish go torpid over the winter north of Zone 9. A deep zone 30″–36″ (c. 80–90 cm) in depth will provide an ice-free refuge for a pool's residents from Zones 8 through 5. However, even a thin layer of ice can inhibit gas exchange. This in turn can lead to mortalities that become evident with the spring thaw. Two simple measures will go far towards eliminating this hazard. The first is to thoroughly clean the pool bottom immediately after the first frost. Remove any dead vegation whose decomposition would remove scarce oxygen from solution and try to pump or siphon off as much of the debris overlying the pond bottom as possible. Then stand a weighted bundle of straw or reeds in the deep end of the pool. This will prevent the surface from freezing over entirely and facilitate gaseous exchange between the air and water. Once these precautions have been implemented, the pond keeper need worry no further about how his fish will fare during the winter months.

Pond keepers living north of Zone 5 have the option of either providing a refuge zone greater than 3′ (c. 1 m) deep for their fish during the winter or, alternatively, of overwintering pool fish indoors. The latter is far and away the simplest solution for the inhabi-

tants of small garden ponds. Coldwater fish adapt quite readily to aquarium life provided one respects their need for more living space than demanded by tropical species of the same size.

The quarters intended for pond fish should be set up at least two weeks prior to the anticipated move indoors. This allows the nitrogen cycle sufficient time to become fully established before the addition of the fish. This is very important as it is rarely practical to introduce the pond fish to their new home a few at a time. Incidentally, there are alternatives to traditional aquaria available as indoor accommodations for large goldfish or nishiki-goi. Small plastic children's wading pools can be set up easily in a corner of the basement, where they provide very economical winter quarters for large pool fish. Because of their large size and messy feeding habits, both of these large cyprinids require power filtration of their indoor homes. Smaller species will prosper under a wide range of filtration regimes. As all coldwater fish have lower tolerances of dissolved carbon dioxide and higher oxygen requirements than their tropical counterparts, supplementary aeration should always be provided to their quarters. All the species considered herein can be overwintered successfully at temperatures from 50°F–62°F (°C–°C). The cool corner of an unheated basement or a room where the thermostat can be set for the high 50°'s are equally suitable locations for a tank of coldwater fish during the winter months.

The first frost of the season marks an opportune moment to bring pond fish in for the winter. Fill several plastic buckets or basins with pond water. Then drain the pond to a depth of one foot (c. 30 cm) and remove any planting containers and accessory structures from the nearly empty basin. The simplest way to capture the fish is with a small seine. Appearances notwithstanding, this approach is far less traumatic to larger fish than pursuing them with a dip net. Fish should be placed in the holding receptacles as soon as they are captured. Provide these vessels with aeration, particularly if the weather is on the warm side or the fish numerous.

If the fish have bred during the summer, the pond keeper will probably find himself with more fish on his hands than he originally stocked. In the face of limited holding space, he must therefore decide which specimens are worth the trouble of saving for next summer. Many native minnows and killifish are short-lived species that seldom survive to breed twice in nature. Large specimens rarely overwinter well and notwithstanding their often impressive appearance, are best passed over in favor of younger conspecifics. Sunfishes, catfish and both goldfish and nishiki-goi are, on the contrary, long-lived species. It is thus sensible to select large specimens for next season's stocking, the more so as they can be expected to overwinter happily indoors. The temptation to bring **everything** inside is great but must be avoided. Coldwater fish respond poorly to crowding. Overstocking invariably leads to severe die-offs with large specimens the first affected. Surplus fish can be returned to the pond after it is refilled to take their chances with the coming winter or given to friends. **They should never be released into natural waters!** Such actions are illegal in most jurisdictions, for they invite the establishment of undesirable exotic species, with all the negative consequences such an event can have on a drainage's ecological balance.

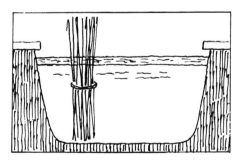

*Bundle of straw to prevent complete icing over and to ensure adequate gas exchange.*

After suitable precautions to bring the temperatures of holding basin and tank into equilibrium have been taken, the fish can be released into their new home. Observe them carefully for signs of parasitic infestation. Pond conditions favor the transmission of skin and gill flukes as well as more readily noted parasites such as anchor worm and fish louse. If the telltale signs of such infections (scratching against the bottom of solid objects, bloody spots of the flanks, rapid breathing, excessive production of body slime) are noted, immediate treatment with the appropriate medication is called for. Several proprietary anti-parasitical agents are commercially available for use on coldwater fish. All give satisfactory results when used according to the manufacturer's instructions. It is also a good idea to put the newly introduced fish on a diet of Tetra's anti-parasite medicated food for seven to ten days after their removal from the pond. This will eliminate any internal parasites they may have contracted during their outside sojourn.

Routine maintenance differs little from that required by aquaria containing tropical fish. Readers wishing to learn more about keeping coldwater fish in captivity are referred to the Tetra Library's **Coldwater Fish,** by Professor Werner Ladiges. The only point that merits particular emphasis touches upon feeding. Because they are kept in cooler water than their tropical counterparts, coldwater fish have less active metabolisms. They therefore require less food. A single feeding daily suffices if the temperature range suggested earlier is maintained. If it is allowed to drop a further 10°F (°C), it may not be necessary to feed the fish more than twice a week.

## Goldfish

To most people, "goldfish" and "pond fish" are virtually synonymous. Goldfish are the oldest of all ornamental pond residents, the first orange-red mutants of the common crucian carp having been cultivated at least as early as the 10th century AD by the Chinese of the early Sung dynasty. By dint of patient selective breeding, dedicated goldfish fanciers in the Far East have established a bewildering selection of varieties that differ from their olive green, short-finned progenitor in every conceivable detail of color, body shape, finnage, scale type and eye development. No other fish

and very few other animals have undergone so thorough a degree of physical modification over the course of their domestication.

Goldfish owe their popularity as pond fish as much to their hardiness as to their pleasing appearance. So long as extremes of pH and hardness are avoided, they prosper under any water conditions. Normal-bodied varieties are reliably winter hardy as far north as Zone 5 and have been known to survive mild winters as far north as Zone 3. As they overwinter well in unheated aquaria, goldfish can even be stocked as summer pond residents north of Zone 5 with great success. Summer temperatures rarely pose difficulties to these less highly selected varieties south to Zone 8, while the provision of a deep, shaded refuge zone and moderate artifical aeration minimizes the risk of losses even as far south as Zone 10.

Allowing for an eventual adult size of 8"–10" (c. 20.0–25.0 cm) SL, goldfish should be stocked at the rate of one specimen/25–30 gallons (100–120 l) of water. If this seems conservative, bear in mind that goldfish breed freely from a length of 4" (10.0 cm) SL onwards. Hence the desirability of a conservative stocking rate that allows for the survival of some fry. With the provision of effective artifical aeration, this stocking rate can be doubled. Bear in mind that the increased carrying capacity thus obtained is purchased at the cost of suitable growing conditions for water lilies. Each pond keeper must decide for himself if this represents a favorable tradeoff.

Goldfish are easily fed. Flake foods such as Tetra's DoroFin and TetraFin are a convenient staple diet for smaller specimens, while pelletized food such as Tetra's Floating Pond Sticks are the most economical means of feeding larger individuals. Goldfish (and most other pond fish) can be easily conditioned to congregate in a given spot at the sound of a bell or hand clap. One need

*Opposite: Of all long-finned goldfish varieties, the comet is best suited for life in the garden pond.*

only give the desired signal before each feeding. Goldfish will supplement their diet by browsing on aquatic invertebrates and algae. Very robust specimens may also nibble soft-leafed aquatic plants but even large goldfish pose no threat to water lilies or lotus.

The usual difficulty goldfish encounter in small ponds is heat stress. They do not appreciate water temperatures greater than 78°F (24°C) and typically display severe respiratory distress when the temperature climbs above 85°F (30°C). In the latter case, only prompt provision of artifical aeration and a reduction in the number of fish present will prevent losses. Abrupt temperature drops can also cause problems for goldfish. Such trauma can trigger an attack of "ich", recognizable as a sprinkling of white dots on the fin and body. Fortunately, "ich" responds well to a number of simple treatments. Proprietary medications such as Tetra's Desa-Fin cure such infestations efficaciously. Chilling can also provoke swim-bladder disfunction in goldfish varieties with foreshortened, "egg-shaped" bodies. Spontaneous recovery sometimes occurs if the affected fish is removed to a vessel filled with just enough warm water to cover its back completely. In many cases, the damage is irreversible, and even if a cure is affected, the recoveree suffers a strong likelihood of a relapse if subsequently exposed to similar stress.

Goldfish under pond conditions can suffer from external parasites. Persistent "scratching" against solid objects or "glancing" off the bottom combined with labored breathing are signs of a fluke infestation. Bloody patches with an associated thread-like structure are indicative of anchor worm. The "thread" is the body of the parasite, actually a crustacean rather than worm. Fish lice are translucent, shield-shaped crustaceans with conspicous eyes, most easily observed when they are feeding near the bases of the vertical fins. Flukes are highly contagious and in themselves can pose a serious threat to the well-being of even large goldfish. Unless present in large numbers, the other two parasites cause, at the most, localized discomfort to their hosts. The puncture wounds they cause

can become secondarily infected, however. Hence the wisdom of eradicating them as soon as they are noticed. Tetra's DesaFin, a broad spectrum anti-parasitical medication, gives satisfactory results against all three parasites when used according to the manufacturer's instructions. Medications that specifically address infestations by both parasitic crustaceans are also commercially available. These are based on

*A typical selection of year-old goldfish. Young specimens such as this are readily available and reasonably priced. Larger specimens can prove considerably more expensive.*

organophosphate insecticides. Hence they must be employed with great care because of their toxicity. Prudence dictates moving the infested fish to a separate hospital tank, should one decide to employ these products in the treatment of either anchor worms or fish lice.

Goldfish attain sexual maturity at 4" (c. 10 cm) SL. They breed freely under pond conditions but fry survival is minimal in the absence of their keeper's intervention. With the onset of sexual activity, males develop a profusion of small, horny white protuberances on the snout and cheeks. Novice goldfish keepers sometimes mistake the sudden appearance of these "pearl organs" for the onset of disease. Similar structures characterize sexually active males of most cyprinids. Their onset is a perfectly normal aspect of these fishes' reproductive cycle and should not be a cause of alarm.

*Both, the common short-finned goldfish (above) and the shubunkin (below) make hardy, colorful pond residents.*

The actual spawning act involves a great deal of chasing and splashing about in the shallows. Inexperienced pond keepers often interpret such activity as a sign of distress. If anything, the reverse is probably true! Techniques of successful goldfish breeding are beyond the scope of this book. Interested readers are referred to Tetra's **Coldwater Fishes** for a useful overview by Professor Werner Ladiges. It is worth observing here that due to the extremely complicated genetics of the more highly selected goldfish varieties, only a minute percentage of the fry produced by even champion breeders will resemble their parents. Maintenance of high quality strains thus requires intense and painstaking culling as well as a great deal of rearing space.

While all goldfish varieties display well in an outdoor setting, they do not thrive equally under pond conditions. Deep-bodied varieties are prone to swim-bladder problems when exposed to the variable water temperatures of a pond at the beginning and end of the growing season, and tend to overwinter poorly in cold climates. They are also more prone to respiratory distress in hot weather than their less highly modified cousins. Varieties that sprout accessory growths on the head, such as lionheads and orandas, are particularly sensitive to lowered oxygen levels. Such varieties as the

*Goldfish varieties such as the lionhead (top) that sport head growth are particularly vulnerable to respiratory stress. The black moor (center) is one of the few goldfish varieties with modified eye developement that can be recommended for the garden pond. Deep-bodied goldfish (bottom) such as this beautiful calico fantail are extremely vulnerable to fish predators such as water snakes and racoons.*

bubble eye and telescope are obviously more prone to eye damage than are normal eyed goldfish, just as veiltails are more vulnerable to torn or nipped fins. Finally, any variety whose modifications interfere with normal swimming ability is **extremely** vulnerable to predators.

The prudent pond keeper thus limits his selection of goldfish to the less highly modified varieties. The so-called common goldfish has unmodified body and finnage, differing from the crucian carp only in its coloration. Its name notwithstanding, the common goldfish is available in a wide range of colors, from crimson to white. The calico or shubunkin is a strikingly handsome multicolored sport of the common goldfish. The comet goldfish has an unmodified body, but a greatly enlarged tail fin. The fantail has a somewhat stockier body than the common goldfish, together with an enlarged double caudal fin and a doubled anal fin. Both calico and solid color comets and fantails are generally available. The black moor is a brassy umber fantail with somewhat protruberant eyes. These goldfish varieties are readily available through commercial channels at reasonable prices. All prosper under pool conditions and their presence is a distinct asset to any ornamental pond.

## Nishiki-goi

Colored carp, or to give them their proper Japanese name, nishiki-goi, stand in the same relationship to the common carp, *Cyprinus carpio,* as the goldfish does to the crucian carp. Outside of Japan, these spectacular pond fish are usually known as koi. This is not an abreviation of nishiki-goi, but rather the Japanese word for carnal love. This unfortunately usage probably arose from a linguistic misunderstanding and is certainly best discarded in favor of a less offensive epithet.

The earliest Japanese references to colored carp date back to the 6th century AD. In the intervening years, meticulous breeders have developed an array of color varieties that puts the goldfish to shame. Three distinct scale types have also been developed, but in body form nishiki-goi remain unchanged from their wild progenitors, unlike their smaller cousins. While some might regret this state of affairs, all will applaud the fact that the most brilliantly colored nishiki-goi is every bit as hardy as his wild relatives. Colored carp overwinter reliably as far north as Zone 5 while withstanding the summer temperatures of Zone 9 and 10 better than goldfish. Like their wild

relatives, colored carp are very long-lived. Life spans in excess of two centuries have been reliably documented for exceptional specimens. With so much going for them, it is no surprise nishiki-goi are giving goldfish a real run for the title of "most popular outdoor ornamental fish".

Their only real disadvantage is large adult size. Specimens routinely grow to 18" (c. 45 cm) SL, and individuals 2' (c. 60 cm) SL are far from unusual. These clearly are not the fish for a small pond. A minimum pond length of 9' (c. 3 cm) is often suggested for a colored carp pond; 12' (c. 4 cm) is probably closer to a realistic minimum. As noted earlier, nishiki-goi grow rapidly under pond conditions. Hence the need to exercise restraint when stocking juvenile specimens.

Because carp have a tendency to stay closer to the bottom than goldfish, some references recommend displaying them in ponds no more than 2' (c. 60 cm) deep. This is unwise for several reasons. First of all, a deeper zone serves as a refuge against both winter ice and excessive summer heat. Such shallow ponds make is impossible to overwinter these fish outside north of Zone 8 and invariably require mechanical aeration during the summer in Zones 8 through

10. They also afford the fish no refuge from such predators as racoons, which can pose a threat to nishiki-goi up to 12" (c. 30 cm) SL. Colored carp are easily trained to come to the surface in response to a fixed signal. It is better to rely upon such behavioral conditioning to bring these fish into view than to house them in dangerously shallow ponds. Colored carp are more herbivorous than goldfish. Taken with their larger adult size, this tendency poses serious risks to most submerged plants. Unless very hungry, nishiki-goi will not molest water lilies. However, because their mode of feeding tends to stir up bottom sediments, most serious fanciers choose to filter their carp ponds to improve viewing conditions. As noted earlier, water lilies do not appreciate significant water movement. Thus it is hardly surprising that they do not prosper under such conditions. Because they hold their leaves clear of the water, lotus do not suffer in the face of power filtration. They also seem to relish the somewhat eutrophic conditions typical of a carp pond. Lotus are thus the ornamental plant of choice for use with nishiki-goi.

Colored carp are voracious feeders. Pelleted foods should constitute their staple diet,

supplemented by "treats" such as *Tubifex,* mealworms and freeze dried plankton. They are quick to learn that the appearance of humans at the pool's edge is usually followed by that of food on the water's surface. It is thus a simple matter to condition them to respond to a fixed signal, such as a bell or a hand clap. Colored carp will also learn to take food from their keeper's fingers and even to "beg" by sticking their heads out of the water and mouthing the air! The appeal exerted by such behavior is obvious, but it is important not to get carried away when dispensing rations to such eager eaters. Overfeeding can cause as many problems in a garden pond as in an aquarium.

The care of nishiki-goi is otherwise as for goldfish. Both species suffer from the same maintenance problems and parasites and should be treated in the same manner when difficulties arise. Like their smaller relatives, colored carp spawn freely under pond conditions. The onset of breeding is likewise marked by the eruption of spawning tubercles on the males heads. The mechanics of spawning are identical to those of the goldfish, save only that the act is accompanied by even more splashing and commotion. Though a large female carp can shed half a million eggs, few will survive the voracity of the breeders long enough to hatch without human intervention. A discussion of nishiki-goi breeding techniques goes beyond the scope of this book. Interested readers are referred to aposite titles in the list of recommended readings that follows the text. As with goldfish, only a small percentage of the fry produced by a spawning pair or trio of colored carp will be of exhibition quality. This is particularly evident in the bicolor and tricolor varieties. Ruthless culling is essential to the maintenance of a quality strain, while by virtue of their greater fecundity, serious culture of nishiki-goi requires even more space than that of fancy goldfish.

Colored carp appear to exist in a bewildering variety of color patterns and scale types, each with its own Japanese designation. First impressions to the contrary, one need not be fluent in Japanese to select nishiki-goi intelligently! The seemingly infinite diversity of phenotypes actually resolves itself into a quite manageable array of five basic color patterns and four basic scale types. As any color pattern can appear in any scale type, it is easy to understand why at first sight colored carp diversity seems so overwhelming.

The simplest of the five color varieties is the so-called solid color nishiki-goi. Here the body is a single color, unrelieved by any accent marks. Solid color nishiki-goi can be red, orange, yellow, gold, white or blue. Next are the three bicolor varieties: white body with red accent marks ("kohaku" in Japanese); light body with black accent marks ("bekko" or "utsuri" depending upon whether lighter colors or black predominate in the overall pattern), and white body with a single red patch on the top of the head ("tancho"). Last of all are the tricolors, either white fish with red and black accent marks on the body ("sanke") or black fish with white and red accents ("showa").

The non-metallic scale type corresponds to the wild phenotype. Metallic scale varieties are characterized by a high lustre, uniformly distributed over the dorsum and flanks. In the diamond scaled varieties, the irridescence is concentrated into discrete points, giving the impression that the fish have been liberally dusted with sparkling highlights. Finally, the so-called German-scaled nishiki-goi are characterized by one or two rows of very large scales running along the back and the mid-lateral line and otherwise naked bodies. Most German-scaled varieties are also metallic scaled, but normal and diamond scaled variants are also possible. Note that all these varieties are equally hardy under pond conditions. This leaves aesthetic considerations as the only basis for choosing between them.

Colored carp do not display to advantage in an aquarium. Hence the importance of viewing specimens from **above** to properly judge their desirability. This is best accomplished in a white enameled pan under natural light. When selecting solid color nishiki-goi, look for intensity and uniformity of color. Avoid fish with a washed out or patchy appearance. The red cap in "tancho" varieties should be large, dark red and symmetrical. In the bicolor and tricolor varieties, look for sharp contrast between the accent

### One-colored Koi

Metallic Ohgon  Koi with a silvery, golden, yellowish, orange or platinum shimmer. Unmixed colors.

### Two-colored Koi

Kohaku        white with red markings.
Hi Utsuri     black with red patches.
Shiro Bekko   white with black markings.
Shushui       blue black and shoulders, red belly.

### Three-colored Koi

Sanshoku      white, red and black (many variations).
Asagi         bright or pale blue. Back with bright blue scales, red marks; the scales have a white brim.

marks and the base color. The more symmetrically disposed the accent marks, the more perfect — and valuable — the specimen. Because no two specimens are alike, large, well-marked show specimens of these bicolor and tricolor varieties can bring amazingly high prices. Japanese — and even some foreign — enthusiasts have been known to pay as much as $ 10,000 for an outstanding show fish!

Both logistic and economic factors usually dictate purchasing young colored carp 3″ to 6″ (7.5 cm–12.0 cm) SL, and allowing them to grow to their full potential in their new home. Japanese-bred specimens are unquestionably the best obtainable through commercial channels. Unfortunately, they are rarely available save on the Pacific coast and are often quite expensive. Hawaiian-bred fish are more readily available and less costly. One can find nice solid color metallic and normal scaled specimens among Hawaiian fish, but as a rule the bicolor and tricolor varieties fall short of Japanese standards. English-bred colored carp are just beginning to enter the North American market. Their quality is excellent and their price competitive with Hawaiian fish. Domestically bred nishiki-goi have considerable potential, but it is virtually impossible to secure quality specimens unless one knows a serious breeder. The fish that enter commercial channels are usually culls and not worth the trouble of buying, notwithstanding their low purchase price. Quality colored carp are not to be had for a pittance regardless of their origins. While their price may well be considerably greater than that of other outdoor pond residents, remember that few investments furnish such a long-term return in grace and beauty as a selection of these colorful charmers.

## Other Eurasian Coldwater Fish

Few representatives of this fish fauna are regularly available to North American pond keepers. Those that are make attractive and interesting additions to the garden pond,

and are well worth the effort of tracking down. Remember, these fish have the potential to become naturalized in most parts of North America. *Past experience with both carp and goldfish suggest such introductions are uniformly detrimental to native fish communities.* Responsible pond keepers should thus make a point of never releasing any exotic coldwater fish into free-flowing waters.

## Orfe *(Leuciscus idus)*

This robust cyprinid is native to much of Europe, occurring as far east as the Ural Mountains. The form usually kept as a pond fish is light gold oligomelanic variety with bright red fins. Orfe are robust schooling fish, capable of attaining a foot (c. 30 cm) SL. They are carnivorous, feeding to a large extent on stranded terrestrial insects. Their penchant for swimming just below the surface in anticipation of such prey keeps them in constant view, which accounts for much of their popularity as pool residents. Unlike many large minnows, the orfe poses no risk to submerged plants.

Orfe prefer neutral to slightly akaline, moderately hard water. They are quite resistant to low water temperatures and can be over-wintered outdoors as far north as Zone 5. This species does not tolerate temperatures above 70°F (c. 20°C) well. Supplementary aeration is thus almost mandatory during the summer months in Zones 7–9, while the culture of the orfe is probably best not attempted in Zone 10. Like most large cyprinids, orfe are greedy eaters. Flake foods are an acceptable staple diet for small specimens, while pelleted foods are a more efficient diet for large individuals. Orfe are subject to the same ills as goldfish under pond conditions and should be treated in the same manner should problems arise.

Provided they are given a cool rest period during the winter months, orfe breed freely under pond conditions. Like all true minnows, males develop conspicuous nuptial tubercles on the head with the onset of sexual activity. They are egg scatters, whose spawning resembles that of goldfish. Pond keepers wishing to breed this species will find the techniques recommended for goldfish culture aposite. The culture of the orfe is prohibited in some jurisdictions. Check with the local office of the state or provincial fish and game authority before making any plans to purchase specimens.

Rudd are still-water fish in nature. They can thus withstand lower dissolved oxygen concentrations than the orfe. Temperatures up to 75°F (c. 24°C) are well tolerated without supplementary aeration. This species will overwinter outside as far as north as Zone 5 without difficulty. Its water preferences, maintenance and reproductive pattern are as given for the orfe. Prudence likewise dictates ascertaining the legality of rudd culture before stocking them in the pond.

## Bitterlings
The bitterlings are a distinctive subfamily (Rhodeinae) of minnows characterized by their unusual spawning behavior. The females of these deep bodies cyprinids deposit their eggs in the gill chambers of freshwater mussels of the Family Unionidae by means of a long ovipositor inserted into the bivalve's excurrent siphon. The brilliantly colored male hovers over the incurrent siphon after the female has shed her

**Rudd** *(Scardinius erythryopthalmus)*
The rudd is another robust, bright silver cyprinid with bright red fins. Growing as large as the orfe, this species is deeper bodied and somewhat less active. It is largely herbivorous in nature, feeding upon soft-leafed submerged plants in captivity. Under pond conditions, neither *Vallisneria* nor lilies need fear its attentions.

eggs and releases his milt. The respiratory action of the mussel carries the sperm into the gill chamber, where fertilization of the eggs occurs. The zygotes complete their development within this protected environment and exit via the excurrent siphon once they become free-swimming.

The subfamily comprises half a dozen genera, most native to eastern Asia. The bit-

*Preliminaries to spawning in the Japanese bitterling, Rhodeus acellatus.*

terling best known in the aquarium litera-ture, *Rhodeus amarus,* is a European spe-cies rarely available to North American aquarists. The Japanese bitterling, *Rhodeus ocellatus,* is frequently marketed here under the name tanago, the Japanese vernacular for these minnows, or Japanese rainbow-fish. Both species live in shallow, often stag-nant, heavily planted waters in nature. They can thus tolerate lower dissolved oxygen concentration than the generality of cold-water fish and can easily cope with tempe-ratures up to 80°F (c. 26°C). Both species are hardy enough to overwinter outside as far north as Zone 6. As they adapt to aquar-ium conditions better than most coldwater species, overwintering them indoors is a simple matter. Bitterlings are not fussy about water chemistry as long as extremes of pH or hardness are avoided, and are sel-dom troubled by diseases or parasites. These vivacious minnows are omnivorous in nature and can be expected to do well on a diet of pond flakes in captivity.

Bitterlings spawn freely in captivity as long as an appropriate host for their eggs is pres-ent. The size of the mussel seems more important in this context than its specific identity. Both the European and Japanese bitterling will spawn freely in an wide range of North American mussel hosts. Unlike the generality of coldwater species, bitterlings enjoy a protracted spawning season. This allows their keeper to enjoy their brilliant coloration all summer long.

### North American Coldwater Fish

North America boasts the richest temperate zone freshwater fish fauna in the world. The number of species suited for life in the gar-den pond numbers in excess of a hundred. Even a cursory review of all these fish is far beyond the scope of this book. The species covered herein are all hardy, colorful, readily available commercially or easily collected from the wild. Equally important, their pos-session is legal throughout the United Sta-tes and Canada. To most economically con-vey relevant information on these fish the following coding has been used:

MS: maximum size given as standard
     length (SL);
TM: maximum temperature tolerated;
P:   predatory on smaller fish.

Collecting native fishes for pond or aquar-ium use is an enjoyable adjunct to fish keep-ing. However, prospective collectors should inquire beforehand about the legal status of their activities. Some jurisdictions require a collecting permit, others restrict the collecting gear that can be used or the waters wherein collecting is allowed. Most restrict the possession of "game" fish and many afford legal protection to rare or threatened species over and beyond that provided by federal statutes. Always contact the local office of the state or provincial Fish and Game Department before going into the field! Even innocent violation of aposite laws can result in stiff fines and confiscation of collecting gear, including, at the presiding judge's discretion in many jurisdictions, the guilty party's vehicle.

A useful reference for the collector of native fishes is the **Atlas of North American Freshwater Fishes.** This comprehensive work gives useful information on the geographical distribution and habitat preferences of North American fishes, cites relevant references dealing with their natural history and indicates those species covered by the U.S. Endangered Species Act. It is published by the North Carolina Biological Survey and can be purchased through that state's Museum of Natural History.

### North American Minnows
*(Family Cyprinidae)*
Most native minnows sport attractive breeding dress but are nondescript for the balance of the year. The two following species owe much of their appeal as pool residents to the persistance of their brilliant coloration throughout the summer.

**Rosy Gold Minnow** *(Pimephales promelas)*
(MS: 4″ (c. 10.0 cm) SL; TM: 85°F (c. 30°C); WH: Zone 2).
The rosy gold minnow is a catatechnic color variety of the fathead minnow developed by Billy Bland's Fishery of Taylor, Arkansas. It thus stands in the same relationship to its wild progenitor as the goldfish does to the crucian carp. Its bright coloration and extreme hardiness make an excellent bait fish. Millions are reared for this purpose yearly, while large numbers also enter the tropical fish trade as "feeder fish". A visit to a bait shop is the simplest way of securing specimens.

The rosy gold minnow is an ideal candidate for small ponds. This species is indifferent to water chemistry as long as extreme pH or hardness values in either direction are avoided. It can tolerate both high summer temperatures as well as low dissolved oxygen levels. It suffers from few diseases or parasites, poses no risk to aquatic plants and greedily takes flake foods in captivity.

Minnows of the genus *Pimephales* deposit their eggs on the undersides of floating objects, the roofs of caves or on vertical surfaces. The male tends the clutch vigilantly, annointing the egg mass periodically with anti-bacterial substances secreted from the spongy dermal swellings on the top of his head. Rosy gold minnows breed freely under pond conditions, and as females mature successive batches a eggs throughout the summer, reproductive activity is effectively continnous throughout the growing season. If well-fed, adult rosy gold minnows are not particularly cannibalistic. The survival of considerable numbers of fry is thus assured so long as no other fish are present in the pond. This is not a long-lived species in nature, and even under less rigorous conditions prevailing in captivity, few indiviuals live longer than two years.

**Red Shiner** *(Notropis lutrensis)*
(MS: 3″ (c. 7.5 cm); TM: 85°F (c. 30°C); WH: Zone 5)
The red shiner occurs naturally in the wes-

tern half of the Mississippi basin as well as in southeasterly draining rivers as far westwards as the Rio Grande. Its popularity as a bait fish has led to its widespread naturalization throughout the southwestern U.S. By virtue of its vivid coloration, the red shiner regularly appears in tropical fish stores under such misleading but descriptive names as Asian or African fire barb! It is both an excellent aquarium and small pond fish. This minnow is unusual among *Notropis* in that reproductive activity is continuous under favorable environmental conditions. Hence males retain their brilliant breeding dress year around under aquarium conditions.

Red shiners inhabit slow-moving, often highly eutrophic streams. They can thus tolerate low oxygen levels and elevated water temperatures quite well. These minnows prefer slightly alkaline, moderately hard water, but tolerate extremely hard, saline water to greater degree than any of their congeners. Acidic conditions are not appreciated. When kept in acid water, this species appears prone to skin parasites and bacterial infections. The red shiner is otherwise a hardy and undemanding species that prospers on a staple diet of flake foods.

*Notropis lutrensis* males defend spawning sites over coarse gravel bottoms but do not actively protect the eggs once they have been shed. In some areas, they spawn in the nests of sunfishes, an arrangement that exploits the parental behavior of territorial male centrarchids. If coarse gravel is used as a top dressing for planters, the fish will

spawn readily thereupon. Alternatively, they can be offered clay flowerpot saucers filled with gravel. Each male will defend such an artificial territory vigorously against others of his sex. Like the rosy gold minnow, this species is not given to cannibalism if well-fed. Substantial numbers of fry can thus be anticipated at summer's end if no other fish are present in the pond. Exceptional individuals can live up to five years in captivity but most do survive their second breeding season.

Many other small native minnows make good pond residents. The genus *Notropis* is particularly rich in brightly colored species. As long as he observes relevant regulations, the pond keeper will find it worth the effort to seek out and collect these highly desirable but underappreciated ornamental fishes.

## North American Catfishes
### (Family Ictaluridae)

Although many ictalurid catfishes will live happily in the garden pond, their somber coloration does little to recommend them to most pond keepers. The one exception to this rule is the albino color form of the channel catfish, *Ictalurus punctatus*. This catatechnic color form of an important food fish has become a popular aquarium resident. Fry from 2″ to 6″ (c. 5.0 cm–12.0 cm) SL are generally available from tropical fish retailers during the late spring and early summer months.

The natural range of the channel catfish is North America between the Rockies and the Appalachians from southern Canada to the Gulf of Mexico inclusive of Florida. It can thus withstand summer temperatures as far south as Zone 10 and will overwinter successfully outdoors northwards to Zone 4. This species tolerates eutrophic conditions well and prospers over a wide range of pH and hardness values. It is troubled by few diseases or parasites and feeds voraciously on pelleted foods.

The chief shortcomings of the albino channel catfish are its large size and piscivorous tendencies. This catfish can grow over a yard (c. 1 m) in overall length in nature, while 18″ (c. 45 cm) SL specimens are not at all uncommon under tank conditions. As they grow longer, albino channel catfish become

*A juvenile albino channel cat.*

progressively more predatory towards smaller pond or tank mates. Individuals a foot (c. 30 cm) SL or larger can safely be kept only with large goldfish and nishiki-goi. Even small speciments should **never** be housed with highly selected goldfish varieties, as they will attack the eyes and fins of their helpless tankmates. Like most heavy feeders, albino channel cats quickly learn to

*The brown bullhead, Ictalurus nebulosus.*

recognize their keeper and can be easily taught to surface at a set signal and beg for food.

The success enjoyed by the channel cat in commercial aquaculture is due in part to the ease with which it can be induced to breed under pond conditions. The egg mass is placed in a cave and carefully cleaned and guarded by the male, who also supervises the mobile fry vigilantly. Albino channel catfish are as easily bred in ponds as their normally colored brethren. However, as they mature somewhere between 12" (c. 30 cm) and 18" (c. 45 cm) SL, relatively few garden ponds are large enough to satisfy their spatial requirements. Hence most pond keepers are content to keep single specimens as pets and leave the breeding of albino channel catfish to professional aquaculturists. Pond keepers who wish to observe the fascinating reproductive behavior of ictalurid catfish are advised to work with the smaller bullheads such as *Ictalurus natalis* or *I. nebulosus*. Widely distributed and easily collected, these smaller icturulids seldom exceed 1' (c. 30 cm) SL. Their cryptic color weighs against them as pool residents. However, their smaller adult size allows them to adapt more readily to the constraints of life in a small pond.

## Native Killifishes
*(Family: Cyprinodontidae)*
Killifish are better known as aquarium than as pond residents. However, most North American species adapt well to pool conditions, breeding freely even in small garden ponds. Operationally, killifish can be divided into bottom-living, midwater-swimming and surface-dwelling species. As limited space precludes a thorough review of the family, one or two representatives of each group will be briefly profiled herein.

## Bottom living killifish
**Flagfish** *(Jordanella floridae)*
(MS: 3½" (c. 8.5 cm) SL; TM: 85°F (c. 30°C); WH: Zone 9)
This chunky herbivore is native to peninsular Florida. It does not prosper in soft, acid water, but is otherwise tolerant of a wide range of water conditions. A typical inhabitant of shallow, heavily planted, often stagnant waters, the flagfish withstands low oxygen concentrations far better than most native pond fish. As it also overwinters happily indoors, there is no reason why pond keepers in the central and northern parts of North America should neglect J. *floridae.* Filamentous algae supplemented by aquatic invertebrates are its staple diet in nature. In captivity, the flagfish relishes flake foods. Flukes can be troublesome when the fish are crowded, but afflicted individuals respond well to standard treatments.
Males defend spawning territories c. 1' (30 cm) square against both male conspecifics and other fishes. Do not stock more males than the bottom area of the pond can afford

territories. Otherwise serious fighting will occur. Neither ought flagfish be housed with long-finned goldfish varieties, whose finnage will certainly suffer from the attentions of territorial males. Depending upon the coarseness of the substratum, the male may or may not excavate a shallow nest. A saucerful of coarse sand is readily accepted in captivity. A male entices a ripe female into his territory, where she deposits a few eggs daily. He defends the accumulated clutch fiercely, and may also engage in rudimentary hygienic behavior towards the zygotes. There is no care of the mobile young. Adults are not overly cannibalistic. Hence many fry will survive in the absence of heterospecific pond mates.

*Male (above) and female of the Coachella pupfish, Cyprinodon macularius californiensis.*

The desert pupfishes of the genus *Cyprinodon,* native to the southwestern U.S. also adapt well to life in the garden pond. These brilliant blue killifish can prosper in the hardest, most alkaline water and tolerate both high and low temperatures better than does J. *floridae.* Their maintenance requirements and reproductive patterns are otherwise identical to those of the flagfish. Pupfishes are not commercially available and must therefore be collected. Many *Cyprinodon* species are protected by state and federal statutes. Hence the importance of ascertaining beforehand whether a given species may be legally collected and kept as a pond resident.

## Midwater swimming killifish

**Bluefin dace** *(Lucania goodei)*:
(MS: 2½" (c. 60 cm) SL; TM: 85°F (c. 30°C);
WH: Zone 9.

**Rainwater Killifish** *(Lucania parva)*
(MS: 2" (c. 5.0 cm) SL; TM: 85°F (c. 30°C);
WH: Zone 5).

The bluefin dace is widely distributed in peninsular Florida, with isolated populations occurring along the coastal plain northward to central Georgia and westward into Alabama. Frequently sold as an aquarium fish, *L. goodei* is usually available through commercial channels. The rainwater killifish is native to fresh and brackish water habitats along the Atlantic and Gulf coasts from Cape Cod southward to the mouth of the Rio

Grande. Native populations occur well inland in west Texas, while naturalized populations of *L. parva* are to be found in several western states. Apart from episodic appearances in bait shops, this species is not commercially available, but it is easily and legally collectible throughout its extensive range.

These peaceful, highly social killifishes are best kept in schools of 6–12 individuals. They prosper over a wide range of water conditions and make ideal residents for small ponds. Highly efficient destroyers of mosquito larvae both in nature and in captivity, they readily accept flake foods. Under crowded conditions, both *Lucania* can be troubled by gill flukes. Avoid medicines containing malachite green when treating these killifish, as both seem sensitive to its presence.

Both *Lucania* species deposit a few eggs daily on fine-leafed aquatic plants. They spawn throughout the summer and can prove quite prolific under pond conditions. Adults will eat eggs, but disregard fry. Considerable populations can thus build up if no other fish are present in the pond. Neither species seems to live more than two years in nature, hence it is best to choose smaller individuals when selecting fish to overwinter indoors.

## Surface dwelling killifish

**Golden Topminnow** *(Fundulus chrysotus)*
(MS: 2½" (c. 6.0 cm) SL; TM: 85°F (c. 30°C);
WH: Zone 7)

**Blackstripe Topminnow** *(Fundulus notatus)* (MS: 3″ (c. 7.5 cm) SL; TM: 85°F (c. 30°C); WH: Zone 5)

While all of the strictly freshwater *Fundulus* species are excellent pool residents, the foregoing combine hardiness, attractive coloration and widespread availability to a greater degree than the majority of their congeners. The golden topminnow occurs in coastal streams from South Carolina to eastern Texas inclusive of peninsular Florida and the southern third of the Mississippi basin. Pond-bred Florida specimens are usually available from tropical fish retailers. The blackstripe topminnow occurs throughout the Mississippi basin from the Great Lakes to the Gulf of Mexico, as well as in coastal rivers as far west as central Texas. It is not available commercially but can be easily collected throughout its range.

Both species inhabit shallow, well-planted biotopes. They prefer neutral to slightly alkaline water but will do well under a wide range of pH and hardness values. Their habit of swimming just below the surface in search of stranded terrestrial insects makes them highly visible in the field and contributes to their appeal as pond fish. *Fundulus* are only weakly social as subadults and grow more solitary as they age. Both sexes of *F. chrysotus* and *F. notatus* are weakly territorial, defending territories c. 3′ (1.0 cm) square in nature. Pond stocking rates should be calculated accordingly. Floating flake foods are eagerly taken both indoors and out. As these fish are carnivorous, high protein foods such as Tetra's Cichlid Flakes should be offered them in preference to the usual pond foods. Neither species is particularly subject to diseases or parasites.

While many *Fundulus* are egg buriers, these two deposit a few eggs daily in fine-leafed submerged plants or the roots of floating plants. Breeding success is unlikely unless the pond is heavily planted, for both sexes will cannibalize eggs and mobile fry. Notwithstanding their small adult size, these topminnows are long-lived fish. It thus pays to select large specimens for overwintering indoors.

### Native Livebearers
*(Family Poeciliidae)*

Poeciliids are also better known as aquarium than as pond residents. Of the four genera native to temperate North America,

*Male of the heteromelanic color morph of Gambusia affinis.*

*Gambusia* is **totally unsuited** for life in a garden pond. All *Gambusia* are voracious predators on smaller fishes, notwithstanding their popular name of mosquito fish. Even worse, they are incorrigible fin nippers capable of reducing the finnage of fancy goldfish to shreds in a few days' time. They should **never** be introduced into an established aquarium or pond, even as food items! The only native *Poeciliopsis* species is protected by the U.S. Endangered Species Act, which puts it beyond the pale for amateur pond keepers. Representatives of the remaining two genera, *Heterandria* and *Poecilia,* are highly desirable outdoor ornamentals.

cousin, the mosquito fish. Fine flake foods are readily taken by *H. formosa* both in ponds and aquaria.

The pygmy livebearer differs from the generality of poeciliids in producing a few fry every three to five days rather than a single large brood monthly. In a well-planted pond with a sizeable marginal zone, most fry will survive to adulthood. Florida populations breed year around, while those from further north reproduce only during the summer months even when housed under favorable conditions indoors. *Heterandria formosa* thrives under aquarium conditions. The ease with which it can be overwintered inside makes it a good pool resident even in those areas north of its natural range.

**Pygmy Livebearer** *(Heterandria formosa)*
(MS: 1¼″ (c. 3.0 cm) SL; TM: 85°F (c. 30°C); WH: Zone 9).

Were it not for its surface-living habits, this diminutive species would be much too inconspicuous to make a good ornamental fish. As it is, it makes a nice addition to the marginal zone of large ponds and an excellent choice for smaller ones. Pygmy livebearers prosper over a wide range of pH and hardness values. They are social little fish best kept in groups of six or more individuals. Like many small fish, they are more comfortable in well planted surroundings. They are largely insectivorous in nature and do as good a job controlling mosquito larvae in captivity as their much less desirable

**Sailfin molly** *(Poecilia latipinna)*
(MS: 6″ (c. 15.0 cm) SL; TM: 85°F (c. 30°C); WH: Zone 9)

This popular aquarium fish has much the same distribution in the U.S. as does *H. formosa* but can be found as far west along the Gulf Coast as the mouth of the Rio Grande in Texas. Its range extends southwards to the western coast of Yucatan in Mexico. Naturalized populations are also reported from southeastern Nevada and the lower Colorado River drainage in Arizona and California, inclusive of the Salton Sea. Sailfin mollies require alkaline, moderately hard water to prosper. If this requirement is met, *P. latipinna* does far better in outdoor ponds than it does under tank conditions. Mollies are

social, but males will fight if crowded. A good rule is one male molly/square meter (c. 1 square yard) of pond surface. Like its congeners, *P. latipinna* is herbivorous in nature. Flake foods are readily accepted both indoors and out, but under pond conditions the fish have the opportunity to supplement their diet by grazing on naturally present algae. Sailfin mollies are prone to the same diseases and parasites as egg-laying killifish and should be treated accordingly.

Mollies are very prolific. Females drop up to 150 robust fry every month. As adults are not cannibalistic if well fed, most fry will survive unless more predatory fish are also in residence. By the standards of most livebearers, *P. latipinna* is a long-lived fish, a factor to be considered when selecting specimens to carry over the winter indoors. This is particularly relevant information in view of the fact that males grow no further after their gonopodia develop from the undifferentiated anal fin. It thus pays to bring only the largest males in for the winter. Numerous catatechnic varieties of the sailfin molly are available as aquarium fish. Apart from the fact that light colored variants are more susceptible to predation than is the wild phenotype, all make very satisfactory pond fish.

### Sunfishes *(Family Centrarchidae)*

Notwithstanding their brilliant coloration, hardiness and interesting reproductive behavior, most sunfishes are too large, aggressive and predatory to make good residents for the garden pond. The happy exceptions are a handful of dwarf species that are every bit as pretty as their larger relatives but have none of their undesirable characteristics.

**Blackbanded Sunfish**
*(Enneacanthus chaetodon)* (MS: 2½" (c. 6.5 cm) SL; TM 85°F (c. 30°C); WH: Zone 6)

*The pumpkinseed, Lepomis gibbosus, grows too large to be a good candidate for small garden ponds.*

**Blue-spotted or diamond sunfish**
*(E. gloriosus)* (MS: 3" (c. 7.5 cm) SL; TM: 85°F (c. 30°C); WH: Zone 5)

**Banded sunfish**
*(E. obesus)* (MS: 3" (c. 7.5 cm) SL; TM: 85°F
(c. 30°C); WH: Zone 5)

The genus *Enneacanthus* is restricted to the Atlantic coastal plain and the peninsular and panhandle of Florida. The most northerly ranging species of the genus, the banded sunfish, is found as far north as southern New Hampshire. The blue-spotted sunfish reaches upstate New York, while the black-banded has never been taken past northern New Jersey. In nature, all three are typical inhabitants of heavily planted, nutrient poor, often very acidic standing waters, where they are often found living together. In captivity, they seem to prefer moderately hard, neutral to slightly alkaline water, and display to advantage only in a well-planted pond. Apart from highly ritualized intermale aggression in conjunction with breeding, these are social fish. Nor are they at all piscivorous, feeding exclusively on aquatic invertebrates in nature. Reports in the literature to the contrary notwithstanding, these sunfishes readily learn to take flake, freeze dried and fresh frozen foods in captivity. Though quite sensitive to nitrogen cycle mismanagement, they are otherwise very hardy and are seldom troubled by parasites.

Like all other sunfish, males of these species construct nests in shallow water at the onset of breeding season in the late spring. They differ in their ability to nest successfully in heavy stands of aquatic plants as well as over bare sand bottoms. Females respond to a male's courtship by depositing eggs in his nest. He then drives them away and assumes the task of cleaning and guarding the zygotes himself. Parental care ceases as soon as the fry are mobile. Spawning activity can continue throughout the summer months. Despite high fry mortality, a few young from each spawning will usually survive to independence from each male's nest.

The virtues of all three species as aquarium subjects has long been recognized. Both the black-banded and blue-spotted sunfishes are routinely available through commercial channels. All three species can be easily and legally collected throughout their extensive ranges. As one might expect, they overwinter well indoors. Bear in mind that these are long-lived, slow growing species when deciding which individuals to bring in for the winter.

**Orange-spotted sunfish**
*(Lepomis humilis)* (MS: 4" (c. 10.0 cm) SL;
TM: 90°F (c. 33°C); WH: Zone 4; P)

The orange-spotted sunfish ranges throughout the Mississippi basin and in Gulf Coast rivers as far east as Alabama and west to central Texas. It is a common inhabitant of disturbed, turbid habitats and prospers over silty bottoms to a greater degree than other sunfishes. This species prefers moderately hard, slightly alkaline water but can tolerate very hard water successfully. The bantam sunfish has much the same habitat preferences in nature as the three

*Enneacanthus* species, but is restricted to the lower Mississippi Valley and rivers of the Gulf coastal plain from eastern Lousiana to central Texas. Like its distant cousins, the bantam sunfish tolerates acidity but seems to prefer moderately hard, neutral to slightly alkaline waters.

**Bantam sunfish**
*(Lepomis symmetricus)* (MS: 2½" (c. 6.5 cm) SL; TM: 85°F (c. 30°C); WH: Zone 3; P)

Both dwarf *Lepomis* are moderately predatory in nature and will take the fry of other species under pond conditions. They certainly prefer live food but quickly learn to take prepared and frozen foods in captivity. These are robust little fishes, seldom troubled by diseases or parasites. Males, however, will fight ferociously over resting sites. A stocking rate of one male per 3' square (c. 1 square meter) of pond bottom is the easiest way of circumventing this problem. The mechanics of spawning resemble those of the genus *Ennaecanthus,* save that males of neither species can nest in dense vegetation. A clay saucer of fine sand is readily accepted as a breeding site under pond conditions. The spectacular coloration and behavior associated with spawning persist throughout the summer. As males are more aggressive in defense of their progeny than are those of the preceding trio of species, it is not unusual to find quite a few fry present in the pond at the summer's end. Both species do well under aquarium conditions. Large specimens of the bantam sunfish are a bit more aggressive than any of the *Enneacanthus* species. This should be borne in mind when selecting fish to bring indoors for the winter.

Neither the orange-spotted nor the bantam sunfish are commercially available. Both can be legally collected throughout their range. Orange-spotted sunfish are common inhabitants of a wide variety of habitats. Finding them is usually a simple matter. Bantam sunfish are often locally abundant but their specialized habitat preferences make them considerably harder to find. All sunfish are sensitive to malachite green. This fact must always be taken into consideration when medicating a pond or aquarium where they are present.

*Though they do well in a garden pond, pygmy sunfishes like these Elassoma everglades are too small to make an effective display.*

The pygmy sunfishes of the genus *Elassoma* also do well in outdoor pools. Though they are hardy fish capable of overwintering outdoors through Zone 6, their small adult size and secretive behavior render them inconspicuous under pool conditions. Thus while they are excellent candidates for the coldwater aquarium, they can hardly be included among the roster of ornamental residents for the garden pond.

### Tropical Aquarium Fish in the Garden Pond

With few exceptions, tropical aquarium fish find summer residence in an outdoor setting agreeable. Indeed, most species can be counted on to breed freely under such conditions if the water chemistry is to their liking. Obviously, if the fish are to play an ornamental role in the garden pond, they must

*The white cloud is really a subtropical rather than a tropical minnow. Hence its ability to prosper in the garden pond.*

measure up to the same criteria of easy overhead visibility as do the coldwater species already discussed. This eliminates many of the smaller species from consideration, not to mention those with cryptic dorsal coloration.

It is important to avoid temperature shock when setting tropical fish out and bringing them back inside. Prudence dictates floating the fish in a large vessel containing water from their former home until its contents come into thermal equilibrium with that of their new surroundings. Although a few species, such as the white cloud *(Tanichthys albonubes)* and red paradise fish *(Macropodus opercularis)* can tolerate lower temperatures, the water at the bottom of the deep zone should measure at least 70°F (c. 21°C)

before any attempt is made to set tropical fish outside. Different species respond differently to sudden chilling, but it is always prudent to plan on moving the fish inside about a week before the projected arrival of the first frost of autumn. Remember that the fish may have contracted parasitic infestations during their summer "vacation" and will in any event require some time to readjust to aquarium life. Hence the need to treat them initially in the manner recommended for newly tanked coldwater fish.

The numerous catatechnic color forms of the swordtail *(Xiphophorus helleri)*, true platy *(X. maculatus)*, variatus platy *(X. variatus)* and shortfinned mollies *(Poecilia mexicana, P. sphenops)* make excellent summer residents of the garden pond. Fancy guppies do not, but unmodified conspecifics positively flourish out of doors. Most labyrinth fishes also look well in such a setting. The gold and blue varieties of *Trichogaster trichopterus* and the bright red form of *Colisa lalia* are particularly ornamental additions to an outdoor pool.

*Macropodus opercularis*

*Opposite: These tropical fish relish a summer vacation in the garden pond. Red Swordtail (upper left), Gold Gourami (center left), Common Guppy (bottom left), Blue Gourami (upper right), Coral Platy (center right), Dwarf Gourami (bottom right).*

*The Texas Cichlid can withstand temperatures down to 50°F (c. 10°C) for a considerable time without suffering severe injury.*

Many cichlids likewise prosper under pond conditions, including the popular *mbuna* of Lake Malawi in areas of hard, alkaline water. The Texas cichlid, *(Heros cyanoguttatus)*, the only member of the family native to the U.S., is another good pond resident. It is less troubled by abrupt temperature drops than most representavies of this lowland tropical group. The gold variety of the Mozambique mouthbrooder, *Sarotherodon mossambicus*, is a superb pond fish for areas where the summer temperatures are too warm to permit the keeping of goldfish. Remember that most cichlids will eat smaller fish. Their space requirements outdoors are no different than they are indoors, so stock them accordingly.

*Two mbuna that prosper under pond conditions: above, Pseudotropheus lombardi (male), below, OB morph Ps. zebra (male).*

*The golden variety of Sarotherodon mosambicus.*

*Water striders of the genus Gerris are harmless and interesting inhabitants of the pond surface.*

## Uninvited Guests and Incidental Visitors

The garden pond offers a host of creatures the specialized environmental conditions they require to survive and breed. Like any other body of standing water, it also serves as the focal point for many other animals whose contacts are of a more casual nature. The majority of these unanticipated additions to the pond ecosystem are completely harmless to both cultivated plants and ornamental fish. Many even add considerably to the charm of a pond and its associated bog garden. A minority of species are unwelcome guests whose activities bode ill for either the water garden or its invited residents. The remainder of this chapter is devoted to a cursory survey of these pond inquilines, with emphasis on appropriate responses to the less desirable of their number.

### Aquatic Insects
Insects are conspicuous residents of the garden pond. Dragon flies and damselflies (Order: Odonata) dart over its surface or perch conspicuously along its margins. Water striders (Genus: *Gerris*) and water

boatmen (Genera: *Notonecta Naucoris* and *Nepa)* scurry about in the shallows, quite oblivious to a human observer. Beneath the surface, the larvae of many more species live out their alloted span, their presence often totally unsuspected by even an observant pondkeeper.

Most of the inhabitants of this teaming world are quite harmless to either ornamental plants or pond fish. Mention has

*Backswimmers or water boatmen of the genus Naucoris are residents of the garden pond.*

*The protensible jaw "mask" of dragonfly nymphs permit them to capture large prey efficiently.*

*Adult dragonflies prey relentlessly on flying insects.*

already been made of the larvae of the delta moth and safe measures suggested to control its depradations on aquatic plants. The aquatic nymphs of dragonflies are formidable predators. In their later growth stages, they can prey upon fish up to 3" (c. 7.5 cm) SL. Larger fish are immune to such attacks while themselves preying efficiently upon early instar nymphs. For their part, adult dragonflies are voracious mosquito predators, each individual capable of devouring several score of these blood-sucking pests daily.

All things considered, the loss of a few fry is a small price to pay for the presence of such vibrant, colorful and emminently useful guests.

The diving beetle (Genus: *Dytiscus)* and the giant water bug (Genus: *Belostoma)* are extremely dangerous fry predators and will even attack adult fish up to 4" (c. 10 cm) SL. They are quite devoid of any aquaristically redeeming features and should be netted out and destroyed as soon as they are noticed. It is particularly important to eliminate diving beetles

*Copulating damselflies. Their nymphs, while predatory, are no danger to fish fry.*

*Male diving beetle (Dytiscus).*

*The grooved wing cases of this individual identify it as a female.*

*The massive curved mandibels of this Dytiscus larva identify it as a formidable predator.*

promptly. Their larvae are, if anything, even more voracious than the adults, and the individuals most likely to show up in a newly set-up pond are females in search of an egg-laying site.

This is as good a place as any to emphasize that a garden pond stocked with fish will not serve as a breeding ground for mosquitos. Their larvae are greatly relished food items and are vulnerable to fish predation due to their need to periodically rise to the surface for air. All fish devour mosquito larvae greedily, their depradations limited only by the accessibility of their prey. Hence, if the pond has an extensive shallow marginal zone, it is prudent to stock a few *Fundulus* or *Heterandria formosa* to patrol this otherwise secure larval refuge.

**Chemical insecticides should never be used on or even near a pond.** These substances are extremely toxic to fish. Even minute amounts washed into a pond can precipitate a major fish kill. Pondkeepers living in areas where aerial spraying is regularly carried out to control mosquitos in adjacent marsh land or drainage ditches should be prepared to cover their ponds with a sheet of plastic to protect their fish from accidental downwind drift of the insecticide cloud. Mosquito control agencies are usually willing to provide information on their spraying schedules to concerned residents of their district.

### Snails

Opinions on the desirability of snails in the garden pond are divided. Their advocates point to their role in controlling filamentous algae, whose unchecked proliferation is both unsightly and a threat to ornamental aquatic plants. Their detractors contend that they are just as likely to become a threat to submerged vegetation themselves by virtue of their extreme fecundity in a predator-free environment. As the control of algae is best managed by limiting the availability of plant nutrients through prudent stocking and planting practices, it is difficult to defend the presence of snails in the pond on utilitarian grounds. Their ability to proliferate explo-

sively is incontestable, as is the difficulty of controlling such population explosions under pond conditions.

On the balance, the smaller, extremely prolific species such as the pond snails (Genera: *Limnaea* and *Physa*) and the common ramshorn snails (Genera: *Planorbis* and *Planorborius*) are best excluded from the garden pond. Their introduction to a pond is in any event usually accidental, by means of egg masses deposited unobserved on the leaves of aquatic plants. This is a very good reason not to bring aquatic plants into the garden pond from the wild. Risk of such accidental contamination is greatly reduced when plants are purchased from a reliable commercial supplier.

Larger snail species such as the Colombian ramshorn *(Marisa rotula),* the widely available mystery snails (Genus: *Ampullaria)* and the Japanese livebearing snail *(Viviparus malleatus)* are, however, interesting pond residents in their own right, while their reproductive patterns are unlikely to result in a population explosion. Attractive albino strains of both the Colombian ramshorn and the common mystery snail *(Ampullaria cuprina)* are readily available and make a nice addition to a pond. Neither species can be overwintered outside north of Zone 9, but both adapt well to aquarium life. They can thus be kept successfully inside during the cold months of the year. The Japanese livebearing snail is winter hardy through Zone 5, but does not do well over the summer months south of Zone 8.

It sometimes happens that despite all precautions, the pondkeeper finds himself face to face with an infestation of pond snails. While commercial molluscicides are available, their use in the garden pond is not recommended. They are based on copper compounds that are toxic to plants as well as snails. The safest way to remove these snails is to trap them out. Simply place a block of slow release fish

*Hardy ramshorn snail, Planorbarius sp. (top).*
*Pond snail, Limnea stagnalis (bottom).*

food in an open glass jar or similar container, then submerge it in the shallow end of the pond. The snails will swarm onto the food block. The jar can be easily removed several times daily and its catch of snails disposed of. Nishiki-goi, *Fundulus chrysotus* and all of the small *Lepomis* species cited earlier prey effectively on juvenile snails. Once trapping has reduced the number of adults to reasonable levels, the addition of a few specimens of such malacophagous fishes will usually prevent a recurrence of this problem.

### Other Invertebrates

Leeches (Order: Hirudinaea) and planarian flatworms (Class: Turbellaria) occasionally make their appearance in the garden pond. The former are parasitic, feeding upon the blood of fishes and amphibians. Their presence is unsightly, but they are rarely numerous enough to pose a serious threat to ornamental fishes. They can be eradicated by treating the pond with a formaldehyde-based antiparasital medication such as Tetra's DesaFin. Planarians are harmless scavengers. Their presence in large numbers signals a superabundance of decaying organic matter in the pond and can be a warning of serious overfeeding. Eliminating their food sources through a conscientious program of pond hygiene is all that is required to eliminate them from the scene.

Sowbugs or pillbugs are moisture-loving terrestrial crustaceans of the genus *Asellus.* They are scavengers, feeding on dead plant matter, and can be quite abundant in the marsh zone of a pond. They are harmless to ornamental plants. Pondkeepers whose property is immediately adjacent to a stream or marsh may discover themselves host to crayfish of the genera *Astacus, Cambarus* or *Procambarus,* depending upon the region of North America where they reside. Crayfish are omnivorous but, as already noted, they can be very destructive of aquatic plants under pond conditions. Large specimens will prey upon fish up to 6″ (c. 12.0 cm) SL, and individuals of all sizes eat fish eggs. They

*Crayfish such as this Cambarus sp. should be removed from the garden pond as soon as they are noticed.*

should certainly be removed from a pond as soon as they are noticed. The best means of eradicating crayfish is to trap them out, using the technique outlined previously in the section on water gardening. Crayfish make interesting coldwater aquarium subjects, but they do not belong in the garden pond.

### Amphibians

A garden pond constitutes ideal amphibian habitat. Hence it is hardly surprising that many of these fascinating animals choose to either take up permanent residence in the water garden or make use of a pool as a breeding site. North America boasts a large and diverse amphibian fauna. Hence the impossibility of affording the group more than passing treatment herein. Emphasis has been given to those species most likely to find a backyard pond a congenial home. However, amphibians have a strong tendency to return to the same breeding sites. Suburban pondkeepers dwelling in recently developed areas of wet lowland forest may thus be surprised by some very unusual visitors to their garden ponds. Refer to the several illustrated field guides listed in the final chapter to identify unfamiliar amphibians and learn more about the group's natural history.

117

The red-spotted newt, Notopthalmus vivi-descens is a fairly common pond visitor in the Northeastern U.S. and Canada. This is the terrestrial, or redeft phase of this species.

The rough skinned newt, Taricha granu-losa, is less secretive than most salamanders.

Adult marbled salamanders, Ambystoma opacum, are basically terrestrial but may use the garden pond as a breeding site.

The tailed amphibians (Order: Caudata) comprise newts and salamanders. The former may have two distinct adult forms, the terrestrial eft and the aquatic newt. The latter do not undergo morphological changes linked with reproduction. All are secretive little creatures that spend most of the daylight hours hidden in moist spots under rocks or logs. Nightfall brings them out to forage and breed, though many species can be observed moving about after a heavy rain during the day-light hours. After an elaborate courtship, the male deposits a spermatophore which the female takes into her cloaca. A few species of lungless salamanders eschew the water and deposit their eggs in moist spots on land. The majority deposit their eggs singly or in small groups in the leaves of aquatic plants or under such objects as stones or water-logged branches. Often the sudden appearance of their tadpole-like larvae with their bright red external gill tufts is the first sign of their presence a pondkeeper notices.

The carnivorous larvae grow rapidly and the larval stage itself is usually brief. If the pond has an extensive marsh zone, a few species such as the red-spotted newt (Notopthalmus viridescens) may remain in the immediate vicinity of the pond after metamorphosis. However, in most in-stances the newly metamorphosed adults return to the woodlands whence earlier came their progenitors. The red-spotted newt is a common resident of the eastern half of North America from southern Canada to the Gulf of Mexico. Herpetolo-gists recognize several distinctive sub-species. Pacific coast pondkeepers often play host to breeding groups of newts belonging to the genus Taricha. Two spe-cies are frequently encountered in subur-ban settings. The rough-skinned newt (Taricha granulosa) ranges along the coast from southern Alaska to central California, while the California newt (T. torosa) is found from northern California almost to the Mexican border along the coast and on the western slopes of the Sierra Nevada in the interior. Both of these red-bellied species are less secretive than the majority of salamanders and are often seen moving about during the rainy season on overcast days. This behavior may arise from the security extremely poisonous skin secretions affords them from predators.

The mole salamanders of the genus *Ambystoma* spend most of their adult lives under cover. Pondkeepers in the eastern half of North America may find themselves playing host to the larvae of two of these boldly patterned species. The spotted salamander, *Ambystoma maculatum,* ranges from Nova Scotia and the southern rim of Quebec and Ontario almost to the Gulf coastal plain. It deposits its egg masses in late winter and early spring. The marbled salamander, *A. opacum,* ranges from central New England and the lower Great Lakes region to the Gulf coast exclusive of peninsular Florida. Females deposit their eggs in late fall and early winter. Unlike the spotted salamander, females of this species usually remain near their eggs until hatching. The large tiger salamander, *Ambystoma tigrinum,* occurs throughout the central portion of the continent from southern Canada to the Gulf of Mexico. Populations also are found along the southern Atlantic coastal plain. This robust species can attain 13" (c. 33 cm) in length. It is more inclined to move about in the open than the preceding two species and prefers to live in proximity to water. Breeding is triggered by the onset of rain and occurs from midwinter to early summer, depending upon locality. The survival of local populations of all three of those mole salamanders has been threatened by the loss of traditional breeding sites due to the effects of acid rain.

The lungless salamanders have, as their name implies, dispensed with lungs and rely instead upon their moist skins as their organ of respiration. These slender, short-limbed salamanders do not have an aquatic larval stage. The eggs, deposited in a moist burrow, hatch directly into miniature versions of their mother, who usually remains to protect the egg mass after oviposition. Adults are attracted to moist habitats and may turn up unexpectedly in the bog garden. The red-backed

The spotted salamander, *Abystoma maculatum,* is another species often found in a suburban setting.

*Desmognathus fuscus,* a lungless salamander that may show up in the marginal zone of a pond.

salamander, *Plethodon cinerareus,* is the commonest lungless salamander in the northeastern portion of the United States and throughout the Atlantic provinces of Canada and the southern third of Quebec and Ontario. It ranges as far south as North Carolina along the coastal plain and to the Ohio River in the midwest. South of these boundaries it is replaced by the slimy salamander, *P. glutinosus* whose range extends northwards to central New York and westward to central Texas. Other lungless salamanders of more localized distribution are native to the Rocky Mountain region and the Pacific coast.

None of the salamanders likely to visit a garden pond poses any threat to its other vertebrate inhabitants. Because in so many instances the survival of these inoffensive and quite interesting creatures is threatened by loss of spawning sites, the pondkeeper should welcome their appearance. By virtue of his efforts, these furtive visitors may be afforded an alternative to the finality of local extinction.

Frogs and toads (Order: Salienta) are far more conspicuous residents of a water garden than their tailed cousins. Many species of frogs will happily colonize a garden pond as adults. Others may prefer to live elsewhere for most of the year, but leap at the opportunity to use the pond as a breeding site. With two notable exceptions, both frogs and tadpoles make innocuous and interesting additions to the fauna associated with a backyard pond. Their aquatic larvae are herbivorous and can be of assistance in the control of attached algae. Adults are largely insectivorous. Their foraging can thus assist in the control of both biting insects and plant pests.

True toads of the genus *Bufo* are terrestrial as adults, entering shallow water only to breed. Their eggs are embedded in amorphous globs of gelatinous material attached to submerged twigs or aquatic plants. The jet black larvae are distasteful to most predators, a characteristic that extends to the adults as well. Their parotid glands produce an irritant that mammalian predators find exceedingly distasteful and, in the extreme case of the giant or marine toad, *Bufo marinus,* even lethal. This may account for the relative fearlessness of true toads when confronted by a human observer. If not molested, adult toads become quite tame and can be taught to take mealworms or earthworms from a person's fingers. Their presence in the bog garden is a distinct asset, for they feed voraciously upon slugs and a wide variety of plant-eating insects.

The most common species pondkeepers in eastern Canada and the northeastern U. S. are likely to encounter is *Bufo americanus,* the American toad. Almost equally common in the northeastern and central U. S. and the Great Basin region is Woodhouse's toad, *B. woodhousei.* The southern toad, *B. terrestris,* is the most common garden resident along the southern Atlantic and Gulf coastal plains, inclusive of Florida while *B. boreas,* the western toad, is typically encountered in such surroundings from southeastern Alaska to Baja California along the Pacific coast and in much of the northern Great Basin.

The tree frogs of the genus *Hyla* will also

*Large specimens of the American toad, Bufo americanus, often become permanent features of a water garden.*

*The ice on the pond surface has barely broken before the spring peeper begins calling.*

make use of the garden pond as an oviposition site. Their egg masses are usually deposited in aquatic vegetation in very shallow water. Adults may take up residence in shrubs or trees near the pond, where they are more often heard than seen. They are often the first amphibians to breed in a given area. The high-pitched whistle of the spring peeper, *Hyla crucifer,* is as certain a harbinger of spring in the northeastern United States and southern Canada as the first robin of the season. Cope's tree frog, *H. chrysocelis,* and the grey tree frog, *H. versicolor* are almost as common and widely distributed in the eastern half of North America as the spring peeper. Along the Pacific coast and throughout most of the Great Basin, the Pacific tree frog, *H. regilla,* takes their place in suburban gardens. Its choruses can be heard from January through August in the southern part of its range, typically after a heavy rain.

The true frogs of the genus *Rana* are the only amphibians whose adults will live in the garden pond proper on a permanent basis. Not all are equally aquatic in their habits or, for that matter, equally tolerant of an ongoing human presence. However, even shy, essentially terrestrial species like the elegant wood frog, *Rana sylvatica,* are not adverse to depositing their eggs in a backyard pool. Like true toads, males of this group call from the water. Breeding aggregations can be very large and their associated chorus of calls almost deafening at times. Fortunately, the breeding season is rarely of more than a few week's duration! Frogs deposit long strands or rafts of eggs in aquatic vegetation, often a considerable distance from shore in deep water. This trait makes it a relatively simple matter to distinguish their spawn from that of toads or tree frogs.

Frogs are unselectively carnivorous. Any moving object small enough to swallow is considered prey. Most frogs are too small to pose a threat to adult ornamental fishes and rarely take fry when alternative invertebrate prey are available. The bullfrog, *Rana catesbiana* and, to a lesser extent, the pig frog, *R. grylio,* are exceptions to this rule. They are both large and unselec-

*Though it will deposit its eggs in a garden pond the wood frog, Raha sylvatica, seldom takes up permanent residence therein.*

*The huge mouth and voracious appetite of the bullfrog, Raha catesbiana, pose a serious threat to ornamental fish.*

*The southern leopard frog, Raha sphenocephala, a representative of the Raha pipiens species complex.*

121

tive enough to pose a serious threat to fishes up to 6" (c. 15.0 cm) SL. The former species is ubiquitous east of the Rocky Mountains from southern Canada to the Gulf coast and has been widely introduced outside of its natural range. The latter is restricted to the Gulf coastal plain and Florida. Neither should be allowed to settle into residence in the garden pond. If the pool is small, they can usually be netted out with a large dipnet. When this alternative is unworkable, sunning individuals are fair targets for either a slingshot or a pellet gun. Both species are intensively hunted as a source of frogs legs, which suggests one means of disposing of such uninvited visitors!

As already noted, the wood frog, found throughout subarctic Canada from coast to coast and extending as far south into the United States as northern Alabama in areas of dense woodland, will often spawn in a garden pond but rarely remains in its proximity thereafter. The green frog, *R. clamitans,* found throughout the eastern United States and southeastern Canada, often shows up in a suburban water garden. However, the most usual colonists of the garden pond are the boldly spotted frogs of the *Rana pipiens* complex. The northern leopard frog, *R. pipiens,* occurs throughout subarctic Canada west to the Rocky Mountains southwards into New England and the upper midwest on into the northern and central Great Basin region. South of this line and east of the Great Plains, it is replaced by the southern leopard frog, *R. sphenocephala.* Save in the extreme southeastern corner of the United States, the range of both species in eastern North America is coterminous with that of the pickerel frog, *R. palustris.* A number of true frogs occur west of the Rocky Mountains, but the majority are localized species and none seems to relish human proximity sufficiently to take up residence in the garden pond.

## Reptiles
Though they are perhaps the most aquatic representatives of the order, turtles sel-

*The plant-eating tendencies of such turtles as this yellow-bellied slider, debar them from residence in the garden pond.*

dom even visit the garden pond, much less take up residence therein. Constant persecution has made them too wary of humans to find their continual close presence comfortable. This is probably for the best, for most turtles have herbivorous tendencies that would otherwise pose a risk to aquatic plants. Strictly carnivorous species such as the snapping turtle, *Chelydra serpentina,* and the softshelled turtles of the genus *Trionyx* are important fish predators whose presence in the garden pond would never be welcome under any circumstances.

Thanks largely to the efficient enforcement of protective legislation, the American alligator, *Alligator mississippiensis,* has increased its numbers dramatically along the Gulf coast and throughout Florida. A parallel trend towards the construction of housing developments adjacent to wetlands has greatly increased the likelihood of human/alligator interactions. The unexpected appearance of an alligator in a backyard pond is thus quite probable in this part of the United States, particularly during spells of protracted drought. As even small individuals pose a threat to ornamental fish, alligators can hardly be considered desirable residents of the garden pond, quite apart from the danger large specimens pose to household pets and children. Because they both enjoy statutory protection and play an important role in wetlands ecology, they should not to harmed but rather captured and released in an area well away from human habitation. As even relatively small alligators have formidable jaws and dentition, this is a task best left to specialists. A call to the local animal control officer or the nearest office of the State Fish and Game Department is the logical response to such a visitation.

Both garter snakes of the genus *Thamnophis* and water snakes of the genus *Nerodia* can inflict serious depredations upon ornamental fishes. A much less frequent, though potentially more dangerous visitor to the garden pond, is the cottonmouth or water moccasin *Agkristrodon piscivorus*. This venomous pit viper differs from the true water snakes and the aquatic garter snakes by its large, diamond shaped head and readily elicited threat display, in which the jaws are opened fully to reveal the contrasting white lining of the snake's mouth and throat. Several water snakes have the same color pattern as cottonmouth, but neither swim with their heads well clear of the water or stand their ground when threatened in the manner already noted. *Cottonmouths are extremely venomous and their bite can prove fatal.* They should only be handled by an experienced herpetologist. Hence the pondkeeper is best advised to contact such a person if he suspects that he is playing host to one of these snakes. A phone call to the biology or zoology department of the nearest university will usually elicit information on the whereabouts of such an individual.

Overall, snakes play an important and highly beneficial role in natural ecosystems. Regrettably, the presence of piscivorous species cannot be tolerated in the garden pond. If arrangements for their capture and removal cannot be made, their destruction is the pondkeeper's only alternative. Snakes are most approachable in the early morning hours, while they are still torpid from the chill of the night, or after eating a large meal. Several sharp blows with a garden hoe or a stout stick are all that is required to do execution once the snake has been located.

*Though more terrestrial in their habits than water snakes, garter snakes like this Thamnophis sirtalis can pose a serious threat to pond fish.*

*Water snakes such as this Nerodia can literally clean out the fish population of a garden pond.*

*The water moccasin, Agkistrodon piscivorous, is a very venomous snake that should never be handled by amateurs.*

## Birds

Fish-eating birds are rarely troublesome in urban or suburban gardens. Kingfishers avoid habitats modified by human activity. In any event, if the pond has been built well away from trees, they pose little risk to its inhabitants, for they require a perching site to fish from. In less heavily settled areas, herons and egrets are a much more serious threat to ornamental pond fish. Passive deterrents such as scarecrows or windchimes are not usually effective in keeping wading birds away from a pond, although the presence of a dog in the yard will deter them in most instances. Once an individual bird has learned that a pool contains food, it will continue to visit it until all its inhabitants have been caught. Faced with such depredations, the pondkeeper who is unwilling to screen over his pond has two alternatives. He can either shift to keeping less conspicuous pond residents such as North American native fishes, whose behavioral adaptations may also increase their chances of survival, or opt for the liquidation of the offending bird by a competent marksman.

As wading birds enjoy some degree of statutory protection everywhere in North America, it is prudent to ascertain beforehand the legality of such an extreme solution.

Apart from the odd misdirected or inexperienced duck or Canada goose, water birds rarely visit garden ponds. The behavior of these birds in other settings suggest that the small size of most garden ponds rather than any distaste for human contact underlies such avoidance. As both ducks and geese devour aquatic plants with relish, their absence in this instance is hardly a matter for regret! On the other hand, a backyard pond draws songbirds like a magnet. They will flock to its edges to drink and use the shallows as a bird bath.

Even in an urban setting, the number of species that regularly visit such an oasis is remarkable. Their presence adds greatly to the pleasure to be had from a water garden.

## Mammals

Cats, raccoons and, to a lesser extent, opossums, pose a threat to ornamental pond fish. Cats and opossums fish strictly from the bank and quickly lose interest if their prey dives below or swims beyond their reach. Raccoons, to the contrary, will enter the pond itself in pursuit of prey and can catch fish quite easily in water up to 2' (c. 60 cm) deep. Screening the pond affords virtually complete protection to its residents, but is costly and rarely acceptable on aesthetic grounds. A refuge zone at least 3' (c. 1 m) deep affords some protection against mammalian predators. Selection of ornamental fish with well-developed swimming abilities also limits the impact of their depredations. The presence of a dog in the yard will deter cats and opossums from visiting a pond. Raccoons are less easily intimidated and even a large dog may be forgiven reluctance to tangle with an adult male or a female with kits.

Raccoons will usually ignore pond fish if offered more conveniently accessible food. Hence many harrassed pondkeepers wind up offering their tormentors what amounts to a nightly bribe to leave the pond in peace! Those unwilling to fall victim to this sort of protection racket have as their only alternative the removal of the offending individuals. As few persons seem inclined to take lethal action against these admittedly appealing animals, the usual option entails capturing the offenders and relocating them elsewhere. Local animal control or Fish and Game Department offices will usually supply live traps and transport captured animals to a release point far enough distant to preclude their prompt return. Even this is not a permanent solution. Raccoons have an excellent directional sense and are known to home reliably. Even if this were not the case, captured animals will usually be more or less promptly replaced by a new set of masked marauders.

Because raccoon predation is apt to be an ongoing problem, the only way to keep its impact within reasonable limits is to afford fish effective refuge from these predators.

*Small, shallow ponds such as this are particularly vulnerable to racoon predation.*

Hence the importance of designing a pond with sufficient water depth to allow the fish to move out of reach. The exercise of a certain amount of common sense when stocking the pond is also called for in suburban or rural areas where these animals are abundant. Any goldfish sporting a foreshortened body or highly modified finnage would be a poor insurance risk in such a setting. It would also be imprudent to stock expensive nishiki-goi under these circumstances. The goldfish varieties previously recommended stand a fair chance of surviving in a raccoon-dominated environment, while their modest price makes replacement less traumatic to the pocketbook should the worst occur. Native fishes are much less vulnerable to raccoon predation and may prove a better choice of pond resident in areas where these animals are known to be troublesome.

# Appendix

## Learning More About Pondkeeping

An introductory work such as this can only touch upon such extensive subjects as water gardening and cold water fish culture. Thus the most useful service the authors can provide to interested readers is a guide to alternative sources of information on these topics. As is the case in the tropical fish hobby, the beginner can avail himself of three complementary sources of information: the reliable retailer, specialty clubs and published references. The balance of this chapter explains how to locate and make use of these resources.

## Retail Suppliers

Finding a local retail pet shop or nursery that deals in coldwater fish, pond supplies and aquatic plants suitable for the water garden is not always a simple matter. Pondkeeping is not as widespread a pastime in North America as it is in Britain and Europe. Hence retailers are sometimes reluctant to carry such merchandise. The difficulty entailed notwithstanding, it is worth the effort to locate such a source of supply. A competent and interested retailer can save the novice pondkeeper much grief by directing him towards products and organisms appropriate to local conditions. There are also obvious advantages to selecting one's own plants and fish rather than relying upon someone else's judgement in such matters.

Fortunately for readers living in areas where retail outlets for pond-related merchandise are lacking, there are a number of suppliers who will ship to customers living outside of their immediate vicinity. The firms listed in the accompanying table are experienced and reliable. They publish informative, well-illustrated catalogs, whose perusal during the depths of winter provides an anticipatory thrill well worth their modest purchase price. All are responsive to customer inquiries and are more than willing to aid the novice in his efforts to establish a garden pond. Given their collective expertise in packing and shipping live plants and animals, no less than the efficiency of the contemporary mail and freight delivery companies, there is every reason to patronize these suppliers when the necessity arises.

# List of Mail Order Suppliers of Pond Products, Aquatic Plants and Coldwater Fish

Lilypons Water Gardens
6800 Lilypons Rd.
P.O. Box 10
Lilypons, MD 21717
Telephone: (301) 874-5133

Lilypons Water Gardens
839 FM 1489
P.O. Box 188
Brookshire, TX 77423
Telephone: (713) 934-8525
(Catalog: $ 3.00)

Paradise Gardens
18 May Street
Whitman, MA 02382
Telephone: (617) 447-4711
(Catalog: $ 2.00)

Slocum Water Gardens
1101 Cypress Garden Blvd.
Winter Haven, FL 33880
Telephone: (813) 293-7151
(Catalog: $ 2.00)

Van Ness Water Gardens
2460 N. Euclid Ave.
Upland, CA 91786
Telephone: (714) 982-2425
(Catalog: $ 3.00)

## Specialty Societies

Joining a specialty organization confers two obvious benefits on the novice pond-keeper. First, and most obvious of all, membership affords one access to the best source of published information on a given aspect of water gardening or cold-water fish culture. Of equal importance is the opportunity to meet other people with the same interests. Access to a group of like-minded hobbyists affords many opportunities for informal but highly useful exchanges of information and can act as a powerful stimulus to a newcomer's involvement in his hobby. The accompanying table lists all the specialty groups whose activities are relevant to pond-keeping. It is unlikely that any one person is likely to be sufficiently interested in all phases of water gardening or coldwater fish culture to join them all but there is no hobbyist who would not benefit from membership in at least one of these groups. Joining one or more of these societies is the best investment the novice pondkeeper can make in the longevity of his hobby.

# List of National Specialty Organizations

The Waterlily Society
Mr. Charles B. Thomas
P.O. Box 104
Buckeystown, MD 21717
Annual dues: $ 15.00
Publications: **Water Garden Journal,**
4 issues/year

Goldfish Society of America
Ms. Betty Papenek
P.O. Box 1367
Southgate, CA 90280
Annual dues: $ 10.00 (U.S.);
$ 15.00 (Canada)
Publications: **The Goldfish Report,**
12 issues/year

Associated Koi Clubs of America
P.O. Box 1
Midway City, CA 92655
Annual dues: $ 8.00 (U.S.);
$ 10.00 (Canada)
Publications: **Koi – U.S.A.,** 6 issues/year

North American Native Fishes
Association
Bruce Gebhardt
123 W. Mt. Airy Ave.
Philadelphia, PA 19119
Annual dues: $ 7.50
Publications: **American Currents,**
6 issues/year

# Subscription Information for Magazines Containing Articles on Water Gardening and Coldwater Fish Culture

**Aquarium Digest International**
Tetra Press
201 Tabor Rd.
Morris Plains, N. J. 07950
Subscription: U.S. $ 8.00/year

**Freshwater and Marine Aquarium**
P.O. Box 487
Sierra Madre, CA 91024
Subscription: U.S. $ 22.00/year

**Tropical Fish Hobbyist**
211 W. Sylvania Ave.
Neptune City, N. J. 07753
Subscription: U.S. $ 15.00/year

**How-to-Do-It Information on VHS**
Having your own garden pond offers a lifetime of enjoyment. In addition to this book, you can obtain detailed how-to-do-it information with a special VHS entitled **Having a Garden Pond.** This program is available in a standard ½" VHS or Beta for home VCR's. To order a copy, just send a check for $ 30.00 to Tetra Sales, 201 Tabor Rd., Morris Plains, N. J. 07950 (please specify VHS or Beta).

## Recommended Reading

The following list of published reference works is by no means comprehensive. A full bibliography of titles dealing with goldfish culture alone would exceed in length most of the chapters of this volume! These titles are readily available and aimed primarily at the beginner. Many include more comprehensive bibliographies that the reader can call upon to guide his research into a given topic. It is also worth noting that articles of interest to the pondkeeper often appear in the pages of *Freshwater and Marine Aquarium* and *Tropical Fish Hobbyist Magazine.* Both of these journals are available across the counter in most tropical fish retail establishments. The new monograph series of *Aquarium Digest International* also boasts titles relevant to water gardening and coldwater fish keeping, i. e. ADI No. 43 "Koi and Fancy Goldfish". Subscription information for all three publications is given in the accompanying table.

Axelrod, H. R. 1973. **Koi of the World.** T. F. H. Publications, Neptune City, N. J. (This lavishly illustrated compendium represents the most useful guide to the many different varieties of nishiki-goi. A substantial but worthwhile investment for the neophyte colored carp fancier.)

Behler, J. L. and F. W. King. 1979. **The Audobon Society Field Guide to North American Reptiles and Amphibians.** Alfred A. Knopf Co., New York. (Fully illustrated with color photos.)

Conant, R. 1975. **A Field Guide to Reptiles and Amphibians of Eastern and Central North America.** Second edition. Houghton Mifflin Co., Boston, MA.

Ladiges, W. 1983. **Coldwater Fish in the Home and Garden.** Tetra Press, Morris Plains, N. J. (Well illustrated and informative. A must for the coldwater fish enthusiast.)

Ledbetter, G. T. 1982. **The Better Water Gardens Book of Patio Ponds.** Alphabet and Image, Ltd., Sherbourne, England. (An English book likely to be very useful to prospective water gardeners with limited yard space. Available through any of the previously listed suppliers.)

Lee, D. S. et al. (Editors) 1980. **Atlas of North American Freshwater Fishes.** North Carolina Biological Survey, Raleigh, N. C. (An absolute must for anyone with an interest in the culture of North American native species indoors or out. Provides information on distribution, size and natural history of all species found north of the Rio Grande. Can be obtained by sending U. S. $ 25.00 to: N. Carolina State Museum of Natural History
Publications Dept.
P.O. Box 27647
Raleigh, N. C. 27611
Supplements dealing with the freshwater fishes of the Caribbean region and Mexico are in preparation.)

Masters, C. O. 1974. **Encyclopedia of the Water Lily.** T. F. H. Publications, Neptune City, N. J. (As its title implies, a comprehensive treatment of the culture and cultivars of the most popular aquatic ornamental plant. Well illustrated in color.)

Matsui, Y. 1981. **Goldfish Guide.** Second edition. T. F. H. Publications, Neptune City, N. J. (A well-illustrated treatment of this most popular pool resident.)

Stebbins, R. C. 1966. **A Field Guide to Western Reptiles and Amphibians.** Houghton Mifflin Co., Boston, MA. (Complementary volume to Conant's treatment of the amphibians and reptiles found east of the Rockies.)

Takeshita, G. Y. 1982. **Koi for Home and Garden.** T. F. H. Publications, Neptune City, N. J. (Excellent beginner's guide to the care of colored carp.)

# Key to the Scientific Names

## Plants

| Common Name | Scientific Name |
|---|---|
| African Crypt | *Anubias lanceolata* |
| Ambulia | *Nemophila sp.* |
| American Lotus | *Nelumbo pentapetala* |
| Anacharis | *Elodea canadensis* |
| Arrowhead | *Sagittaria latifolia* |
| Blue Iris | *Iris versicolor* |
| Bog Lily | *Crinum americanum* |
| Cabomba | *Cabomba caroliniana* |
| Canna | *Canna var.* |
| Cattail | *Typha latifolia* |
| Dwarf Cattail | *Typha minima* |
| Dwarf Cyperus | *Cyperus sp.* |
| Dwarf Papyrus | *Cyperus haspans* |
| Elephant Ear, Taro | *Colocasia esculenta* |
| Floating Heart | *Nymphoides peltata* |
| Hornwort | *Ceratophyllum demersum* |
| Japanese Lotus | *Nelumbo nucifera var.* |
| Lizard's Tail | *Saururus cernuus* |
| Marsh Marigold | *Caltha palustris* |
| Milfoil | *Myriophyllum sp.* |
| Narrow-leafed Cattail | *Typha angustifolia* |
| Parrot's Feather | *Myriophyllum aquaticum* |
| Peace Lily | *Spathiphyllum floribundum* |
| Pennywort | *Hydrocotyle vulgaris* |
| Pickerel Rush | *Pontederia cordata* |
| Purple Waffle Plant | *Hemigraphis colorata* |
| Radicans Swordplant | *Echinodorus cordifolius* |
| Red Iris | *Iris fulva* |
| Red Ludwigia | *Ludwigia natans* |
| Sagittaria | *Sagittaria sp.* |
| Scarlet Altenanthera | *Altenanthera reinickii* |
| Siberian Iris | *Iris siberica* |
| Spike Rush | *Eleocharis montevidensis* |
| Sweet Flag | *Acorus calamus* |
| Umbrella Palm | *Cyperus alternifolius* |
| Vallisneria, Tape Grass | *Vallisneria spp.* |
| Water Arum | *Peltandra virginica* |
| Water Hyacinth | *Eichornia crassipes* |
| Water Lettuce | *Pistia stratoides* |
| Water Lily | *Nymphaea var.* |
| Water Poppy | *Hydrocleys nymphoides* |
| White Arum | *Peltandra sagittifolia* |
| Yellow Water Iris | *Iris pseudoacorus* |

# Animals

| Common Name | Scientific Names |
|---|---|
| American Alligator | *Alligator mississippiensis* |
| American Toad | *Bufo americanus* |
| Backswimmers | *Notonecta spp.* |
| | *Nepa spp.* |
| | |
| Banded Sunfish | *Enneacanthus obesus* |
| Bantam Sunfish | *Lepomis symmetricus* |
| Bitterling | *Rhodeus amarus* |
| Blackbanded Sunfish | *Enneacanthus chaetodon* |
| Blackstripe Topminnow | *Fundulus notatus* |
| Bluefin Dace | *Lucania goodei* |
| Blue Gourami | *Trichogaster trichopterus var.* |
| Blue-spotted Sunfish, | |
| Diamond Sunfish | *Enneacanthus gloriosus* |
| Brown Bullhead | *Ictalurus nebulosus* |
| Bullfrog | *Rana catesbiana* |
| California Newt | *Taricha torosa* |
| Channel Catfish | *Ictalurus punctatus* |
| Coachella Pupfish | *Cyprinodon macularius californiensis* |
| Colombian Ramshorn | *Marisa rotula* |
| Cope's Treefrog | *Hyla chrysocelis* |
| Crayfish | *Astacus spp.* |
| | *Cambarus spp.* |
| | *Procambarus spp.* |
| | |
| Diving Beetle | *Dysticus sp.* |
| Dwarf Gourami | *Colisa lalia* |
| Flagfish | *Jordanella floridae* |
| Garter Snakes | *Thamnophis spp.* |
| Giant Water Bug | *Belostoma sp.* |
| Golden Topminnow | *Fundulus chrysotus* |
| Goldfish | *Carassius auratus var.* |
| Gold Gourami | *Trichogaster trichopterus var.* |
| Green Frog | *Rana clamitans* |
| Grey Treefrog | *Hyla versicolor* |
| Guppy | *Poecilia reticulata* |
| Japanese Bitterling | *Rhodeus ocellatus* |
| Japanese Livebearing Snail | *Viviparus malleatus* |
| Marbled Salamander | *Ambystoma opacum* |
| Mosquitofish | *Gambusia spp.* |
| Mozambique Mouthbrooder | *Sarotherodon mossambicus* |
| Mystery Snail | *Ampullaria cuprina* |
| Nishiki-goi, Colored Carp | *Cyprinus carpio var.* |
| Northern Leopard Frog | *Rana pipiens* |
| Orange-spotted Sunfish | *Lepomis humilis* |
| Orfe | *Leicuscus idus* |
| Pacific Treefrog | *Hyla regilla* |
| Paradise Fish | *Macropodus opercularis* |
| Pickerel Frog | *Rana palustris* |
| Pig Frog | *Rana grylio* |
| Platy | *Xiphophorus maculatus* |

| | |
|---|---|
| Pond Snails | *Limnaea spp.* |
| | *Physa spp.* |
| Pumpkinseed | *Lepomis gibbosus* |
| Pygmy Livebearer | *Heterandria formosa* |
| Pygmy Sunfish | *Elassoma evergladei* |
| Rainwater Killifish | *Lucania parva* |
| Ramshorn Snails | *Planorbarius spp.* |
| | *Planorbis spp.* |
| Red-backed Salamander | *Plethodon cinerareus* |
| Red Shiner | *Notropis lutrensis* |
| Red-spotted Newt | *Notopthalmus viridescens* |
| Rosy Gold Minnow | *Pimephales promelas* |
| Rough-skinned Newt | *Taricha granulosa* |
| Rudd | *Scardinius erythryopthalmus* |
| Sailfin Molly | *Poecilia latipinna* |
| Shortfin Molly | *Poecilia mexicana* |
| | *Poecilia sphenops var.* |
| Slimy Salamander | *Plethodon glutinosus* |
| Snapping·Turtle | *Chelhydra serpentina* |
| Soft-shelled Turtles | *Trionyx spp.* |
| Southern Leopard Frog | *Rana sphenocephala* |
| Southern Toad | *Bufo terrestris* |
| Sowbug | *Asellus spp.* |
| Spotted Salamander | *Ambystoma maculatum* |
| Spring Peeper | *Hyla crucifcr* |
| Swordtail | *Xiphophorus helleri var.* |
| Texas Cichlid | *Heros cyanoguttatus* |
| Tiger Salamander | *Ambystoma tigrinum* |
| Variatus Platy | *Xiphophorus variatus var.* |
| Water Boatman | *Naucoris spp.* |
| Water Moccasin | *Agkistrodon piscivorous* |
| Water Snakes | *Nerodia spp.* |
| Water Strider | *Gerris spp.* |
| Western Toad | *Bufo boreas* |
| White Cloud | *Tanichthys albonubes* |
| Wood Frog | *Rana sylvatica* |
| Woodhouse's Toad | *Bufo woodhousei* |
| Yellow Bullhead | *Ictalurus natalis* |

# Index

Page citations given in bold face indicate illustrations

# Photographs

(a = above, b = below, l = left, r = right)

Baensch: 67
Barker: 118 m., 123 m., b.
Brünner: 74 b.r., 75 (4), 82 b.r., l., 83 (5)
Castro: 104 r., 105 r.
Frickhinger: 65, 70 a.l., b.l., 72 b., 73 b.l., 74 a.l., 86, 114 b.
Herlong: 68 (2)
Kahl: 82 a.r., 90, 91 a., 92 m., 97, 106 a.l., 109 r., 111 (5)
Kenney: 108 l., 118 a., b. 119 (2), 120 (2), 121 (3), 123 a.
Komai: 92 b.
Law: 92 a.
Lilypons: 39 (6), 40 (6), 70 a.r., b.r., 73 a.l., a.r., b.r., 74 b.l., 79 (6), 80 (6)
Linke: 113 b.
Loiselle: 98 r., 99, 100, 101, 102 a., 103 r., 104 a.l., b.l., 106 b., 107 a.r., 108 r., 109 l., 110 b., 111 b.r., 112 (4)
v. d. Nieuwenhuizen: 98 l., 107 l.
Norman: 110 a.
O'Malley: 117, 122
Paffrath: 74 a.r.
Paysan: 89, 91 b., 103 l., 113 a., 114 a.r.
Reinhard: 102 b., 115 a., 116 a.
Sammer: 8, 114 a.l.
Sluyter: 60 (3), 61 b.r.
Stehling: 42, 55, 126
Terceira: 105 l.
Tetra: title, 9, 20, 31, 35, 50, 61 l., a.r., 62, 64, 71, 72 a., 76, 85, 94, 125
Wieser: 6, 11, 46, 53, 54, 77
Wischnath: 115 m., b., 116 b.
Yoshimara: 96 (8)
Zukal: 82 a.r. (blossom), 107 b.r.

# Drawings

Tscheschner, except 13–19 and 37 (Riepe)

## Above Ground Ponds

A alternative method of creating a water garden is to employ a wooden frame to support a pond liner above ground level. There is nothing new about the idea of growing water plants in free-standing containers. Cut-off wooden barrels have been used to this end for decades. However, their restricted surface area severely restrict the selection of ornamental plants that can be successfully planted in such containers. Furthermore, their shape can make it difficult to incorporate them successfully into many garden designs. Neither of these limitations applies to frame-and-liner ponds, which can be contructed in a wide range of shapes and sizes. They can thus be easily incoportated into any landscaping scheme, while offering the water gardener the possibility of cultivating an extremely wide range of subjects. Such free-standing ponds are ideally suited to small yards or to decks. They thus open the world of water gardening to urban dwellers.

One of the greatest advantages of such frame-and-liner ponds is that their extreme portability. This greatly simplifies integrating such a pond into a yard's existing landscaping. Portability notwithstanding, it is important to keep a few basic rules in mind when choosing a location for a free-standing pond. First of all, the surface upon which it rests must be perfectly level. Second, it is important to keep the lighting requirements of its intended planting in mind when deciding on its eventual location. Finally, it is not a good idea to situate a free-standing pond too near the eaves of a building, as the run-off from the roof can wash noxious substances into it, with predictably disagreable consequences for its inhabitants.

If the pond is intended to sit on a deck, take care to ascertain beforehand that it can supoort the weight of such a volume of water. Water weights just over 8 ibs/gallon (1 kg/1). A free-standing pond a meter square and a meter deep thus weighs 1000 kg (c. 2250 lbs.) when filled. This is a great deal more than even the heaviest pieces of outdoor furniture! To determine the weight of a free-standing pond, one must initially ascertain its volume. This value can be calculated for ponds of the three most popular configurations using the following formlae:

a) square or rectangle
   volume = length x width x depth
b) hexagon
   volume = [(length of longest side x width) + (length of shortest side $^2$)] x depth
c) circle = 3.174 x radius $^2$ x depth

Remember, use the inside length and width of the frame when calculating the volume of quadrangular and hexagonal ponds and the inside radius when calculating that of circular ponds. If the calculations have been done in metric units, divide the volume in cubic centimenters by 1000 to obtain the weight of water in kilograms. If they have been done in Anglo-American units, multiply the volume in cubic inches by .035 to obtain the weight in lbs.

Wooden pond frames require a bare minimum of hardware to construct. However, access to a table saw and a bench-mounted drill are required to do the job properly. While a simple frame takes minimal skill to construct, reasonable expertise in woodworking is required to put together an attractive and functional rim for such a pond. Propsective pond keepers who lack the skills or equipment to construct such a frame themselves will be pleased to learn that complete do-it-yourself kits are usually available at large nurseries or home and garden centers. Failing this, they can be ordered from the suppliers listed in the Appendix.

In the interests of economy, pond frames are usually constructed of pine. It is customary to stain the timbers whatever shade fits most harmoniously with the garden's pre-existing decor. This is more easily accomplished before the frame is assembled than after. This is also the time to treat the timbers with polyurethane varnish. As with any other piece or outdoor furniture, a pond frame holds up much better if it is given a waterproof finish from the start.

The accompanying illustrations detail the assembly of a pond frame and the installation of the pond liner therein. Note that as is the case when installing a liner in a pre-dug hole, all the corner folds should point in the same direction. It is preferable remove any superfluous liner material from view by folding it so that it lies completely under the edge of the frame's rim. If the ammount of overlapping liner material is too great this may not prove practical. It will thus be necessary to trim the edge of the liner after it has been installed. Before cutting any material from the liner, fill the pond to the half way mark, make certain that it fits snugly against the interior of the frame, then staple it to the top of the uppermost course of timbers. Allow a 5.0 cm (2") overlap when trimming the liner. Once the excess liner has been cut away, fold the overlap under and set the rim assembly on top of it. Most pond frames are so designed that this ornamental edgework will hold the liner securely in place once it has been bolted to the main body of the frame.

The extreme portability of a free-standing pond greatly simplifies winter care in areas having a rigorous climate. Simply drain the pond, then either bring the empty receptacle inside or cover it with a tarpaulin or sheet of plastic until the return of clement weather. In those areas with a mild winter climate, a free-standing pond requires the same sort of care as a sunken installation.